Emotional Eating

Eating

Crack the Code of Food Addiction Recovery.

Find the Solution to Binge Eating Disorder and Overeating.

Practical Guide with Workbook

MARY KNOX

Table of Contents

Introduction

Thank you for purchasing and taking the time to read this book. Enclosed is a wealth of information about emotional eating and many strategies and tips for how to conquer it. If you think you may suffer from emotional eating and that it is affecting your life in negative ways, this book will not only help you to determine if this is something you do, but it will also help you to take steps to recover from it. If you have been looking for a place to start, you have found it. This book was made to help you without judgment and without shame. I am determined to help people suffering from the effects of emotional eating one step at a time. In this book, you will find information about emotional eating and how it can affect your brain and your body, some reasons why people emotionally eat, how to tell the difference between actual hunger and emotional hunger, how exercise can benefit people who tend to emotionally eat, as well as a workbook and a meal plan to help get you started by helping you take action. Deciding to read this book is the first step, and you have already begun.

First, we will begin by defining emotional eating. Some of you reading this book may be unsure of whether or not this is something that you suffer from. Emotional eating occurs when a person suffering from emotional deficiencies of some sort, including lack of affection, lack of connection, or other factors like stress, depression, anxiety, or even general negative feelings like sadness or anger, eats in order to gain comfort from the food they are eating. Many people find comfort in food and when this occurs along with negative feelings, and in order to reduce them or to feel better about them, this is called emotional eating. Now, some people do this on occasion like after a breakup or after a bad fight, but when this occurs at least a few times a week, this is when it is considered to have a negative impact on one's life and is when it needs to be addressed.

The next term we will define before jumping into the book is food addiction. While not all those who emotionally eat have a food addiction, they can be seen together quite often. Food addiction is a behavior that involves the consumption of foods that are high in fat, sugar or salt, in other words, that taste great, as these will cause the person to feel rewarded by the chemicals in the brain that these foods release. Consuming these foods in order to feel the reward to a compulsive level is a food addiction.

Binge eating disorder is another disorder that can be seen along with emotional eating. Binge eating disorder is when a person eats much more than a regular amount of food on a single occasion or sitting. And they feel unable to control themselves or to stop themselves. This could also be defined as a compulsion to overeat. In order to be considered a disorder, it has to happen at least two times per week for longer than six months consecutively.

Binge eating is overeating, although this can also be seen separately. Overeating is when a person eats more than they require in order to live and when they consume much more than they need in a day or in a single sitting. Overeating does not necessarily become binge eating, but it can be. Overeating is a more general term for the variety of eating disorders that we just defined. Thus, overeating could involve binge eating, food addiction, or other food-related disorders. In this book, we will be focusing mostly on emotional eating, but keep these additional terms in mind as well as much of the time they will overlap and can be seen together.

With any of these above issues related to food and eating, the reason that they occur is that eating foods that we enjoy makes us feel rewarded on an emotional level within our brain. We will revisit this later on in the book, but keep this in mind for now. If you are wondering why a person would continue to eat when this is known to cause problems in their life. The reason for this is because of this reward that they feel, which encourages them to eat more and outweigh the possible future negative consequences.

Now that we have defined these terms, we are ready to dive into our examination and discovery of the foods that make us feel rewarded, what they can do to our bodies and how we can intervene in this process in order to begin recovery. The problem with emotional eating, or an addiction to food, and what makes it so difficult is that we need food in order to live, and we must eat multiple times a day, every day. This is unlike any other addiction where the person must stop drinking or using a drug altogether, as a person who is recovering from a food addiction must continue to eat. Be gentle with yourself throughout this process as it will be uncomfortable at times and will require strength. This book will help you through it, as you are not alone. I hope that this book also reminds you that many other people are suffering from the same type of food-related disorders as you are and that you are not alone in that either. This book will take a step-by-step approach, which will make for the highest chance of recovery. If at any time you need to take a break in order to think about the information you have learned, feel free to do so, but make sure you come back to this book quite soon after. Going through this process of recovery can be a lot, but with the right support, it will be possible.

Chapter 1: Industrial Foods and Their Ingredients

In this chapter, we will look at the foods that are sold and marketed to us, which are not considered *whole foods*. Whole foods are things like fruits, vegetables, lean meats, and things like this that are not created in a factory. The foods we will be looking at are called *industrial foods*. Industrial foods are foods that are processed and made commercially, such as in a factory or some other process of mass-production. These foods include convenience-made foods like pre-packaged foods, snack foods, or foods that are sold to us in fast-food restaurants. These foods are quick consumption foods that are made to be easily prepared or consumed immediately. We will look at the common ingredients in these foods and the reasons why they taste so great to humans. We will look at what they do to our bodies and why they are not the best option for us.

Industrial Food Production and Ingredients

Industrial food production is all about convenience, speed, and ease of production, sale, and consumption. These foods are not made with the people who will consume them in mind. They are made with the dollar in mind and are marketed towards us as if they are a good option to save time and still eat all of our meals. We will now look at the most common ingredients you can find in industrially produced foods and what these ingredients actually are. Many times we may see ingredients on the packages of foods we eat, but we aren't really sure exactly what they are, just that they taste good. In this section, we will go deeper into them.

MSG

MSG stands for Monosodium Glutamate, which sounds way too sciencey for many of our brains to even pronounce, let alone know what it is or what it does. MSG is added to foods to give it a delicious flavor. It is essentially a very concentrated form of salt. What this does in foods such as fast-food, packaged convenience foods, and buffet-style food is that it gives it that wonderfully salty and fatty flavor that makes us love these foods so much. Companies put this in food because it comes at an extremely low cost, and the flavor it brings covers up the not-so-great flavor of all of the other cheap ingredients that are used to make the food.

MSG has been known to block our natural appetite suppressant chemicals that normally are released when we have had enough to eat. Therefore, when we are eating foods like this, we do not recognize when we are satiated, and we continue to eat it because it tastes so great.

Casein

The next ingredient we will look at is called Casein. This is a heavily-processed ingredient that is derived from milk- this is where it is naturally found. It is processed a few times over and eventually create milk solids that are concentrated. This is then added into things like cheese, french fries, milkshakes, and other fast and convenient packaged or fast-food joint foods that contain dairy or dairy products like pastries and dressings. Casein actually is addictive in itself, and this makes the food it is added to quite addictive for us.

High Fructose Corn Syrup

High fructose corn syrup is surely an ingredient you have heard of before or at least one that you have seen on the packaging of your favorite snacks or fast foods. While this is actually derived from real corn, after it is finished being processed, there is nothing corn-like about it. High fructose corn syrup is essentially the same thing as refined sugar when all is said and done. It is used as a sweetener in foods like soda, cereal, and other sweet and quick foods. The reason why this ingredient is seen so often is that it is much cheaper than using sugar and is much easier to work with.

Food Coloring

Many different food colorings are used in processed foods to give them the visual appeal that will make them look appetizing and make people buy them. The problem here is that these dyes are chemicals that we do not need to be consuming and have been known to cause children to become hyperactive. These dyes are included in mass-produced foods because without them, we would see that most of these processed foods actually look quite unappealing and of sort of greyish-brown color after all of the processing, additions of chemicals and before they have been colored. For example, much of the time when we see a package of "brown bread" we think that this means it is healthier for us. This is not necessarily true, though, as sometimes the brown bread is actually just white bread or bread with processed flour and many additives that has been colored brown so that we as consumers think it is healthier for us.

Preservatives

There are so many preservatives in our foods today and so many different names for them that only the most advanced scientists could pronounce. Preservatives are added to foods in order to keep them fresh for longer or to increase their shelf life. If you have ever seen videos or articles about heavily-processed foods that are laughing about how twenty years from now, they will still look exactly the same, and will not have become moldy or decayed at all, this is because of the preservatives added to it. The longer things will last, the more preservatives they have added into them. If you buy fruit or vegetables regularly, you will know that after about a week or so in the fridge, they start to become moldy and decay. This is what a whole regular food would do, but an industrially processed food would not.

Fat, Salt, and Sugar

Now for the trifecta- fat, salt, and sugar are often seen as a triad in the most processed foods. Even if you think a food is very salty, like a fast-food french fry, there are most definitely heaps of sugar added into it as well. While these three being found together make for a great taste for our taste buds, they are not so great for the body. When finding them all together in a single food item, this is what makes your body crave the food over and over again. Fat, salt, and sugar can be found combined as High-Fructose Corn Syrup, as we talked about previously, or as oils that have been hydrogenated or processed heavily. These two ingredients are cheap and flavorful, so they are added to just about everything we buy in fast-food restaurants or heavily processed foods. If you go to a regular sit-down restaurant, they may not be using only industrially-processed foods, but they will be sure to use a large amount of sugar, fat, and salt together in a single dish which is what will make the food taste great and will keep you coming back again and again.

Why Are These Foods Addictive?

Now that we have gone through the ingredients that you will see most commonly in industrially-produced foods, we will look at their addictive nature and the chemicals and processes in the body that actually make this happen.

To begin, we will return to Casein, the milk-derived ingredient that has highly addictive properties. Casein has been compared to nicotine in its addictive properties. It is often seen in cheese, and this is why there is increasing evidence that people can become, and many are already addicted to cheese. The reason for this is during digestion. When cheese and other foods that contain casein are digested, it is broken down, and one of the compounds that it breaks down into is a compound that is strikingly similar to opioids- the highly addictive substance that is in pain killers.

Combining fat and carbohydrates in foods, such as potato chips, pizza, french fries, among others, has been shown to make these foods even more difficult to resist than other foods that do not contain these similar combinations.

High Fructose Corn Syrup has also been shown to be highly addictive. This substance has been shown to be similar to cocaine in its addictive properties.

The reason that these foods are addictive is their chemical structure. A chemical structure is like the organization of the molecules that make something what it is. Everything has its own chemical structure or its own specific arrangement of molecules, and this is what makes everything different from each other, but some things similar. If two things have very similar chemical structures, they will be similar substances, materials, or objects. So, these addictive chemicals that are found in industrially-produced foods are built of a chemical structure that is very similar to the chemical structure of highly addictive drugs like cocaine, heroin, or opioids. Either this or they break down in our digestive system, and then this process creates chemicals that are very similar to the chemical structure of drugs that are highly addictive. So, to understand why these specific chemical structures are addictive, we will have to understand the science of our brains in a little bit more depth. The next section will go deeper into this so that we can understand that we are very susceptible to food addictions, especially of very specific types of foods.

How Are These Foods Like Drugs

As I mentioned previously, the chemicals that are found in foods like High Fructose Coren Syrup, Casein, Fats, and Salts contain chemical structures that eventually will travel to our brains. When they get there, they find very specific places to rest. These places are built like a puzzle, so these chemicals find their matching puzzle piece in the brain, and they stick to it tightly as their structures fit together perfectly. This is the same with drugs. When we ingest an opioid, like oxycodone, which is a narcotic, this opioid makes its way to the brain and does the same thing. It will look for its matching puzzle piece and link to it tightly. The problem is because the chemicals in food and the substances that are highly addictive drugs are very, very similar. These will find the exact same puzzle pieces as each other. Because of this, they make us feel the same way as each other.

The way that they make us feel is happy, giddy, elated, and like we are having a great time. This feeling is what keeps people who are addicted to these drugs like painkillers or cocaine going back to them for more. This is where the addiction to these drugs comes from. It is more than a conscious decision to continue, but the pursuit of these wonderful feelings that come from a very real chemical reaction in our brain.

Why does this chemical reaction make us feel so good? This is because these drugs act as a reward for the brain and the body. When these chemicals—be they drugs or food additives—find their matching puzzle pieces within the brain, this matching of pieces causes another chemical to be released by the brain. This other chemical that is released is what then makes our brain feel like it has been rewarded. The rewarding feeling makes us feel accomplished, happy, and excited. As humans, receiving the feeling of reward is very strong and very addictive. Every time our brain has this puzzle piece matching, we feel a sense of reward. And whether this comes from a drug or a food additive, our brain can't tell. All our brian knows is that there has been a chemical connection, and it then releases the reward chemical. This is why these addictions are so hard to break. When it comes to drug addictions, people seem to understand that there is something more than the person's willpower involved, and it is something that must be fought hard in order to overcome. The thing that is less understood is that when it comes to food addiction, this is the exact same thing. By explaining this chemical process to you in this chapter, I hope that this helps you to understand why you have a difficult time stopping yourself if you suffer from binge eating, or why it is so hard to say no when you feel like turning to food as a comfort.

Sugar

We will now look more closely at sugar and the ways in which it affects our bodies and our minds. Sugar is actually the worst culprit of all of these food additives. This is because it is so hard to avoid! Sugar is found in everything we eat that we can buy from a restaurant or a store. There are so many forms of sugar and so many names that it is usually disguised in the ingredients list on food packaging. One food may contain 70 percent sugar, but on the label, it may look as if this is not true because the different types of sugar have all been separated in order to trick us into thinking this is not the case. When it comes to avoiding sugar, it takes diligence and a keen eye for detail.

We already discussed one form of sugar, High Fructose Corn Syrup. This type of sugar is cheap and easy to use and is added to virtually everything packaged that we can ingest. This is because it gives even salty foods that tasty flavor balance.

Sugar as a Drug

As we talked about previously in this chapter, the chemicals found in food act in our brains in a very similar way to the way in which highly addictive drugs act. Sugar itself acts in a specific way that makes it so difficult to avoid. Sugar affects what is called the *Limbic System.* A limbic system is a group of structures in the brain that has to do with our emotions and our memory. This includes the regulation of our emotions and forming memories, which contributes to our learning. What this means is that when we eat something very sugary, the chemicals that make up the sugars can affect our emotions. When this happens, it makes us feel emotions like happiness and satisfaction. Then, because eating certain foods makes us feel like this, we form a memory of this, and in turn, we learn that eating these specific foods gives us positive emotions. This makes us keep coming back for more.

So, when we eat something that contains both sugars and Casein, for example, we will get action on our limbic system as well as on our reward system in the brain. Therefore, foods that give us both a feeling of reward and a surge of positive emotion are the most difficult to resist.

And the first ones we turn to when we want comfort in the form of food because we know they will make us feel good. And they always do, as these chemical reactions in the brain occur each time. We may not even realize this, as it becomes second nature to us. We may not recognize the positive feelings we get after we eat something that comforts us, but for some reason, we know we keep craving it. If this has ever happened to you, you now know why this is. After learning about these things, pay attention to your cravings and see if this may be the explanation for why you have them. Pay attention also to the times that these cravings occur. Did you just receive some terrible news? Was it on a rainy day when you were feeling especially down? Hold onto this information as we will revisit it shortly. Later on in this book, we will also be discussing several ways to overcome these challenges to break the cycles of emotional eating and overeating.

The YoYo Blood Sugar Effect

We will now discuss something known as the yo-yo blood sugar effect. This is something that happens in our bodies when we consume too much refined sugar. This is becoming a problem in today's societies as the amount of sugar we regularly consume is more than ever before. This is causing problems for people like type 2 diabetes, obesity, and heart problems. The reason that sugar causes this is the following;

When we consume regular sugar, like natural sugars found in fruits, for example, our body has to transform it through digestion into a simpler form of sugar that can travel through our blood and give us energy. It does this in a controlled way at a steady pace that is perfect for the amount of sugar we need in our bloodstream. However, when we eat sugars that are refined—like white sugar and high fructose corn syrup—this sugar already comes in this simple form that is carried through the blood. This means that the body doesn't have to transform it, and it is already able to enter the bloodstream. When we eat this type, it goes directly into our blood, and this makes for a sugar overload. This is called a blood sugar spike. Our body then can't use up all of the sugar fast enough, and it starts to cause a sort of back up in the bloodstream. In order to try to deal with this, the body releases a hormone that is called insulin. Insulin is likely something you have heard of before. What insulin does it take the extra sugar in the blood and send it to be stored for later, when we need energy. Now, this wouldn't be too terrible if it happened once in a while, but the problem is that when refined sugar is consumed over and over again, this begins to become a bigger problem. When our body receives a quick and massive insulin spike, it lowers blood sugar by a larger amount than it usually would after a regular meal, in order to counter this large spike and prepare itself for a possible overload of sugar. It does this because its main job in the body is to maintain a normal level of blood sugar. After this blood sugar drop that the high levels of responsive insulin cause, we will have a middle to low blood sugar level. When we then eat something sugary again, our blood sugar will spike once again, and the body will react accordingly once again. This effect is called the yo-yo blood sugar effect.

The yo-yo blood sugar effect is hard on our cells and our organs, as it makes them work overtime, trying to compensate for the high levels of refined sugar that we are putting into it. This puts stress on our organs, cells, and body systems and eventually can make them weaker. The other part of the body that sugar negatively affects is the brain. Since the rest of the body is working so hard to accommodate the spikes and dips in blood sugar levels, the brain still needs fuel. While it would usually get fuel from the food, the body is working hard to process; if the body is processing refined sugars, there are no nutrients to send to the brain. This means that it must be fed some other way, and this is done through stored nutrients from other meals. If there are no stored nutrients, though, there is no fuel for the brain, and this makes for reduced efficiency of your brain.

Having sugary drinks on an empty stomach, for example, can cause a large blood sugar spike, starting the day off with a sugary muffin, or having a midnight snack that is full of sugar will also cause this yo-yo blood sugar effect. This is because when your body is in a fasted state, which means that there is no food that it is digesting currently, the processes that control our blood sugar are resting. When there is a massive influx of sugar then, the body's blood sugar-regulating processes were not already in the works, and they will have to not an only startup, but work even harder than normal because the food that has just entered the body is high in refined sugar. The body makes these levels drop to deal with this and thus begins the yo-yo effect of blood sugar.

This yo-yo of blood sugar levels can lead to rapid changes in mood and rapid rises and falls in energy levels. If you have ever felt a "sugar high," and then shortly after felt like your energy levels fell drastically or you "crashed," this is the effect that you were feeling.

All of the factors stated above are the reasons why we should be aware of the amounts of refined and processed sugars we are putting in our bodies and when we are doing so. As we move onto the next chapter, take what you have learned in this chapter with you, and we will build upon this as we continue.

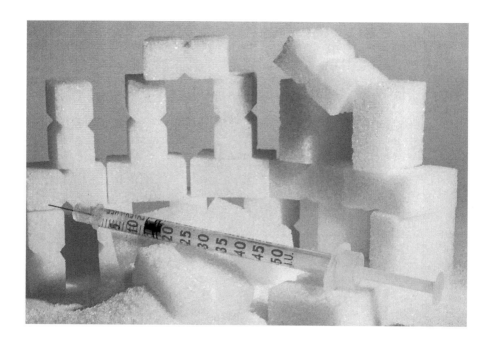

Chapter 2: Diet Changes

We will now discuss several ways that we can begin to combat the cycle of emotional eating and make better and healthier choices for our bodies. The first topic we will discuss is the ways that we can replace industrial foods with better options for our health. We will then look at the cravings we experience and what information we can gather by looking at these more deeply.

Replacing Industrial Foods in Your Diet

We will begin by looking at some common industrial foods that may be in your diet. Think of the foods you reach for when you want something quick and convenient, or when you feel like you want some type of comfort food. These are likely industrial foods and not whole foods.

Sugary Industrial Foods

The first category we will look at is those sugary foods we all know and love. These foods are things like pastries, cakes, cookies, cereals, candy, and anything else that is sweet.

Salty Industrial Foods

The next category is salty foods like potato chips, microwave pizza, french fries, popcorn, crackers, tv dinners, and instant noodles.

Industrially-Produced Drinks

There are a lot of beverages that we turn to for a good taste and a comforting feeling, as well. These include sodas, juices, milkshakes, yogurt drinks, coffee-flavored drinks, sports drinks, cocktails, and energy drinks.

Easy Food Swap Examples

Now that we have examined some common examples of the foods you may reach for when you want a quick snack or a quick comfort, we will look at some common foods that you can replace these with that will be a better option for your health and your brain.

When you are craving candy- like gummies, try instead of having some dried fruits. Dried fruits will have quite a similar texture to gummies and will still be sugary. The difference, though, is that dried fruits contain natural sugars like all fruits contain, so these will be much better for you than refined sugars. The sugars in fruits are the type that your body must convert in order to send it to the bloodstream (like we discussed earlier), so this will not cause a dramatic spike in your blood sugar.

When you feel like you really want the fizzy texture of a soda, try reaching for soda water instead. While it will not be nearly as sugary as soda is, it will have the same texture and mouthfeel, which is part of why we love sodas anyway. In time, you will enjoy the fizzy liquid even if it doesn't contain heaps of sugar.

If you crave sugary foods in general, and there isn't one specific sugary food you are after, try eating fruits. Fruits are sweet, but, as we discussed, they are sweet in a much more natural way than the convenient sugary foods we love. Further, they are just as convenient as these foods as all we need to do is open the fridge, and they are ready to be eaten.

If you enjoy those sugary marshmallow cereals, you don't have to cut out cereal altogether. Try having a healthier cereal with nuts and seeds, which will give you vitamins and minerals, or granola instead. These usually contain some dried fruits for sweetness and a variety of nuts and seeds for texture and nutrition. The milk mixed with cereal will still feel the same in your mouth as those sugary cereals, but this type will be much better for you as long as it doesn't have any added sugar.

If you love potato chips, try eating some roasted vegetables instead. Roasted vegetables can still be a little bit salty, and they will be savory, but they will be much less fatty than potato chips. If you want that crunch, try baking very thin slices of vegetables like yam or sweet potato, and lightly salt them with a little bit of sea salt. This will give you a very similar texture and crunch as potato chips, but it will be a much healthier option for you.

If you love salty popcorn, try something like roasted pumpkin seeds or a nut mix. This will be similar to popcorn in that it contains many small and savory pieces, but nuts contain nutrients that our body can benefit from.

What Do Your Cravings Mean?

We will begin by defining a craving. A craving is an intense longing for something (in this case, a food) that comes about intensely and feels urgent. In our case, that something is a very specific type of food usually. When we have cravings for certain foods, it can actually mean more than what it seems. While we may think that this just a means when we are feeling hungry, or we enjoy the type of food we are craving, this may actually indicate that we are low on certain vitamins or minerals in our body, and the body thinks that we can get it from a particular food, so it tells us that we want that food. The body is trying to help itself by telling you what to eat, and to us, this feels like a craving. The problem is, sometimes, the things we crave won't actually be the best way to get the vitamins or minerals that we need. Having the nutrients that we need in the right amounts in our body helps it to regulate our mood, our hunger, and our cravings. So, when one or more of these nutrients are low, it is hard for us to regulate our appetite and our cravings, and this is why we tend to crave foods that are not actually the very best ways to receive these nutrients. Below, we will now look at some common food cravings and what they can mean for our bodies and our levels of essential nutrients and vitamins.

Chocolate and Magnesium

When we crave chocolate, it is said that this means our body is low on magnesium. Chocolate contains high levels of magnesium, but only if it is dark chocolate. When we crave chocolate, though, it is usually in the form of a doughnut or a chocolate bar, which is the form of chocolate that contains lots of sugar, fat, and oil. Next time you crave chocolate, it may be because of a magnesium deficiency. Other signs of a magnesium deficiency can include general sugar cravings. The problem, though, is that when we consume sugar, our body uses magnesium in order to process it. Therefore, we crave sugar and sugary chocolate, but if we give in to this craving, we may actually end up depleting our already low magnesium stores even more, which can make us crave chocolate and sugar all over again, and the cycle would continue without us being any the wiser.

Chocolate itself is actually quite rich in nutrients; however, it is the actual cocoa that holds all of these nutrients. Therefore, if you are going to eat chocolate to ease your craving and your need for magnesium, make sure that it is dark chocolate, at least 70%, or more in its cocoa content. Cocoa contains high levels of magnesium, iron, fiber, and antioxidants, so while you are getting your magnesium fix, you will also be getting your fill of other good nutrients that your body needs. If you have low magnesium levels, there are many different ways you can get it as well. Eating nuts (like almonds and cashews) or beans are a great choice as they are high in magnesium and may give your body exactly what it needs. If you crave chocolate, try eating these magnesium-rich foods at your next meal, and your craving for chocolate may just dissipate.

Hydration

If you are craving juice or pop or other sugary drinks like this, consider that you might actually be dehydrated and, therefore, thirsty. Sometimes we see drinks in our fridge, and since we are thirsty, we really want them. Sometimes though, we are actually just in need of water, and this would be the best thing to quench our thirst, but these other drinks are always going to be much more appealing to us than water. Next time you are craving a sugary drink, try having a glass of water first, then wait a few minutes and see if you are still craving that Coca-Cola. You may not want it anymore once your thirst is quenched.

Salty Foods

If you are craving salty foods like chips or pizza, you might be low on the element sodium. We must be careful with this one as being low in sodium is actually quite rare given our modern diets. It could be, however, if you sweat a lot that you are low on sodium. If this is the case, though, try reaching for something more natural like celery, milk, or even beets. While these may seem like odd sources of sodium as they don't taste particularly salty, these three foods actually contain natural sodium within them, and they are not nearly as bad for the body as industrial foods are.

Meat

If you are craving meat, you may feel like you want some fried chicken or a hot dog. This can indicate a deficit of iron or protein. The best sources of protein are chicken breast cooked in the oven, and iron is best received from spinach, oysters, or lentils. If you think you may not like these foods, there are many different ways to prepare them, and you can likely find a way that you like. As long as they are not fried, this will be much better for you than a hot dog or fried chicken. The other way to get iron is from lean beef, which can mean eating a lean steak.

Craving meat can also mean that you lack vitamin b12. Vitamin B12 is found in meat and other animal products. What Vitamin B12 does it help us to have a healthy bloodstream and good memory. To get this, you want to eat good sources of meat like organic meats as well as eggs and turkey.

Calcium

We have talked about cheese previously, and how it can actually be addictive because of the casein it contains. If you find yourself craving cheese, it could be because of these addictive properties, or it could be because of a Calcium deficit. In order to find out which of these it is, you need to try eating other foods that are rich in calcium and see if your craving dissipates. Calcium-rich foods include tofu or leafy green vegetables like kale, spinach, or arugula. There are also some forms of cheese that contain good amounts of calcium, and that does not include additives and preservatives. Examples of these include mozzarella and feta cheese.

Fatty Foods

If you find yourself craving fatty, carbohydrate-dense foods like muffins or high-fat baked goods, you could actually have an omega-3 deficiency. Omega-3 is a type of fatty acid, which is usually found in oils or fats. These specific types of fatty acids are called "essential fatty acids" because the interesting thing about omega-3, is that our bodies actually cannot make it themselves. This is what makes it essential, which means that we must ingest it in order for our bodies to have enough. This is why many people take Omega-3 supplements, or you may see eggs sold in the grocery store that have omega-3 written on the packaging. So, if this is the case, what foods should you be eating in order to get this essential nutrient? Omega-3 occurs in fish such as salmon and tuna, or nuts and seeds like walnuts, flax seeds, or chia seeds- those types of seeds that you hear about being added to smoothies or smoothie bowls. Adding these foods into your diet can help you to get this essential nutrient.

Crash Diets

If you have been on crash diets such as extreme low carb diets or liquid-only diets and you have cravings for foods such as carbohydrates, sugars, or fatty foods, this may indicate multiple deficiencies. If you have been drastically limiting your intake of any group of foods like carbohydrates or any type of sugar entirely, you may be missing out on some things that you need like the nutrients described above. The best way to ensure you are getting all of the nutrients you need is by having a balanced and healthy diet. We will revisit this idea later on in the book when we look at more specific approaches to change.

In this chapter, we looked at different cravings and what they can mean, as well as some alternatives to your favorite craving-heavy foods. We will now talk about the best approach and mindset to change and look at some strategies you can use to get started on your journey to a healthy relationship with food.

Chapter 3: The Right Approach To Change

In this chapter, we will look at the best approach to take when it comes to making a change in your life. When trying to make a lifestyle change or trying to change habits that are firmly ingrained in your day to day life, the approach you take will play a large part in whether you succeed or relapse. This chapter will pave the way for you to start taking real action and start taking steps toward a new lifestyle.

Why a Rigid and Aggressive Approach Doesn't Work

When it comes to making any sort of change in life, the approach you take will make or break your success. If you choose an approach that doesn't work well with your specific personality, the likelihood of relapse occurring will be extremely high. In this chapter, we will discuss the drawbacks of approaching change with an aggressive and rigid approach.

Taking an approach that is focused on perfection leaves you feeling down on yourself and like a failure most of the time. Because this causes you to notice that you are not perfect instead of focusing on the good parts, the progress you have made will always make you feel like you are not doing enough or that you have not made enough progress. Since you will never achieve perfection as this is impossible for anyone, you will never feel satisfaction or allow yourself to celebrate your achievements. You must recognize that this will be something complicated, but that you will do it anyways. If you force yourself into change like a drill sergeant and with an aggressive mindset, you will end up beating yourself up every day for something. Forcing yourself will not lead to a long-lasting change, as you will eventually become fed up with all of the rules you have placed on yourself, and you will just want to abandon the entire mission. If you approach the change with rigidity, you will not allow yourself time to look back on your achievements and celebrate yourself, to have a tasty meal that is good for your soul every once in a while, and you may fall off of your plan in a more extreme way than you were before. You may end up having a week-long binge and falling down into worse habits than you had before.

Your mindset plays a huge role in your success when it comes to change. The way that you view your journey will make or break it and will determine whether or not your change is lasting or fleeting, and whether or not you really become invested in making the changes in your life. While you need to push yourself in order to do anything hard, the key is knowing when to ease up on yourself a little bit and when to push harder. Recognizing and responding to this is much more effective than putting your nose to the grindstone every day and becoming burnt out, tired, and left without any more willpower. In order to continue on the long and challenging journey that a lifestyle change involves, you must give yourself a break every now and then. Think of this like running a marathon, where you will need to go about it slowly and purposefully with a strategy in mind. If you ran into a marathon full-speed and refused to slow down or look back at all, you would lose energy, stamina, and motivation in quite a short amount of time and turn back or run off the side of the road feeling defeated and as if you failed. Looking at this example, you can see that this person did not fail. They just approached the marathon with the wrong strategy and that they would have been completely capable of finishing that marathon if they had taken their time, followed a plan, and slowed down every once in a while to regain their strength. Even if they walked the marathon slowly for hours and hours, eventually, they would make it over that finish line. They would probably also do so feeling proud, accomplished, and like a new person. This is how we want to view this journey or any journey of self-improvement. Even if you take only one tiny step each day, you are making a step toward your goal, and that is the important part.

The Deprivation Trap

There is a term when it comes to dieting that is called The Deprivation Trap. The deprivation trap is something that can occur when you approach dieting with a strict mindset. What this means is that you become stuck in a type of thinking trap within your mind. In this type of thinking, you become focused on what you can't have and what you are restricting yourself of. You become hyper-focused on everything you can't allow yourself to have and become resentful of the fact that you aren't able to just eat what you want. After a while, because you are focusing so intently on what you can't have and the fact that you can't have it, you decide that you are just going to have it anyway, or just have a little bit of it, out of a feeling of anger and entitlement. This sense of entitlement. The next thing you know, you have gone on a binge, and after restricting yourself completely for some time, you have now undone that in a single sitting. You will then begin to feel terrible about yourself and what you have done, and you begin to feel like you need to punish yourself. Thus can start the cycle of deprivation.

Further, it is quite difficult to avoid this when you are trying to make a change by using deprivation. It is quite rare that a person, no matter how strong their willpower, will be able to deprive themselves of something without easing off of it completely. A sudden and strict deprivation is not natural to our brains and will leave us feeling confused and frustrated.

How to Overcome the Deprivation Trap

To avoid the deprivation trap, or overcome it if you are already finding yourself there, there are things that we can do and approaches we can take that will set us up better for success.

In order to avoid this trap, the first thing we must do is avoid complete deprivation of anything. Instead of depriving ourselves of something completely, we will instead try to make better choices, one meal or one snack at a time. Focusing on small parts of our day or smaller sections of our lives will help us to motivate ourselves. This is because looking forward to the rest of our lives and thinking that we will never be able to have a certain thing again is quite an overwhelming thought, especially if this is something that we really enjoy. Therefore, we must instead look at it like "I will make a better choice for my lunch today," and then all you need to focus on is lunch, not the entire rest of your life.

Strategies for the Body

We are going to explore some strategies that will help your body to transition away from the choices you have been making and toward new and healthier ones. As we discussed when talking about cravings and what they mean, certain cravings can indicate certain things. When our body is low on some nutrients like Magnesium or Omega-3's, we will also experience things like a foggy brain, less control over emotions, and less willpower. Because we are lacking nutrients and also because we are intaking a high level of sugar through industrial foods, we experience a less than normal level of brain function and mental sharpness. Because of this, it is harder to say no to our cravings, and the cravings don't subside because we are giving in to them and thus still not giving our bodies the nutrients it needs.

In order to break out of this cycle, we will need to begin to make healthy choices and replenish these nutrients that we are lacking. In the last chapter, I described some alternatives to the snacks that are commonly turned to for comfort or that we tend to crave. By choosing these instead of the snacks we crave or desire, we will begin to reduce the amounts of chemicals and sugars in our body and in our bloodstream. Also, as we do this, we can start to add into our diets the foods that will give us the nutrients we need, such as salmon or fish for Omega-3's, or red meat for iron. By taking both of these steps, we will be able to return to our regular level of brain functioning and mental sharpness, which will allow us to resist cravings better and consciously choose healthy and nutritious options. Having that mental sharpness will also include more mental toughness and willpower, as well as the ability to see better the long-term rewards that will come of your current efforts.

Strategies for the Mind

Like we discussed, easing into a lifestyle change is the best way to go about something like this because of the way that our minds work. We don't like looking forward to our lives and feeling like we will have no control over what we are going to do with it. By choosing smaller sections to break it up into, we can be more present in each moment, which makes making healthy choices easier. By doing so, all of these small sections add up to weeks, months, and eventually years of healthy options, and eventually, we have gone a year without turning to sweets in a moment of sadness and only chosen them when we are consciously choosing to treat ourselves.

Another strategy that we can use for our minds is to reward yourself at milestones along your journey. At one week you can reward yourself with a date night at a restaurant, or at one month you can visit the new bakery down the street. This not only helps you to stay motivated because you are allowing yourself some of the joys you love, but it also keeps you motivated because you are allowing yourself to take time to look back at how far you have come and feel great about your progress. Allowing yourself to celebrate goes hand in hand with this, as well. When you make a good choice or plan what you will order at a restaurant before you get there, allowing yourself to feel happy and proud is very important. By doing this, you are showing yourself that you have done something great, that you are capable of making changes, and that you will allow yourself to feel good about these positive strides you have made instead of just looking to the next one all the time. If you were to ignore this and be of the mindset that nothing is good enough, you would end up feeling burnt out and quite down about the length of the process. Think of that marathon analogy again, and this is what can happen if we don't allow ourselves time to feel proud and accomplished for small victories along the way.

Another strategy for the mind is to avoid beating yourself up for falling off the wagon. This may happen sometimes. What we need to do, though, is to focus not on the fact that it has happened, but on how we are going to deal with and react to it. There are a variety of reactions that a person can have to this. We will examine the possible responses and the pros and cons below:

One is that they feel as though their progress is ruined and that they might as well begin another time again, so they go back to their old ways and may not try again for some time. This could happen many times over as they will fall off each time and then decide that they might as well give up this time and try again, but each time it ends the same.

Two, the person could fall off of their diet plan and tell themselves that this day is a write-off and that they will begin again the next day. The problem with this method is that continuing the rest of the day as you would have before you decided to make a change will make it so that the next day is like beginning all over again, and it will be very hard to start again. They may be able to begin again the next day, and it could be fine, but they must be able to really motivate themselves if they are to do this. Knowing that you have fallen off before makes it so that you may feel down on yourself and feel as though you can't do it, so beginning again the next day is very important.

Three, similar to the previous case, the person may fall off, but instead of deciding that the day is a write-off, they tell themselves that the entire week is a write-off. And they then decide that they will pick it up again the next week. This will be even harder than starting again the next day as multiple days of eating whatever you like will make it very hard to go back to making the healthy choices again afterward.

Four, after eating something that they wish they hadn't, and that wasn't a healthy choice, they will decide not to eat anything for the rest of the day so that they don't eat too many calories or too much sugar, and decide that the next day they will begin again. This is very difficult on the body as you are going to be quite hungry by the time bed rolls around. Instead of forgiving yourself, you are punishing yourself, and it will make it very hard not to reach for chips late at night when you are starving and feeling down.

Number five is what you should do in this situation. This option is the best for success and will make it the most likely that you will succeed long-term. If you fall off at lunch, let's say, because you are tired and in a rush and you just grab something from a fast-food restaurant instead of going home for lunch or buying something at the grocery store to eat, this is how we will deal with it. Firstly, you will likely feel like you have failed and may feel quite down about having made an unhealthy choice. Now instead of starving for the rest of the day or eating only lettuce for dinner, you will put this slip up at lunch behind you, and you will continue your day as if it never happened. You will eat a healthy dinner as you planned, and you will continue on with the plan. You will not wait until tomorrow to begin again, and you will continue as you would if you had made that healthy choice at lunch. The key to staying on track is being able to bounce back. The people who can bounce back mentally are the ones who will be most likely to succeed. You will need to maintain a positive mental state and look forward to the rest of the day and the rest of the week in just the same way as you did before you had a slip-up. One bad meal out of the entire week is not going to ruin all of your progress, and recovering from emotional eating is largely a mental game. It is more psychological than anything else, so we must not underestimate the role that our mindset plays in our success or failure.

How to Be Gentle With Yourself

It is important to be gentle with ourselves because we are usually our own toughest examiner. We look at ourselves very critically, and we often think that nothing we do is good enough. We must be gentle with ourselves so as not to discourage ourselves, put ourselves down, or make ourselves feel bad about what we are working so hard to accomplish. We must remind ourselves that everything in life is a process and does not happen instantly, and we mustn't tell ourselves to "hurry up and succeed," as we often do.

When you fall off track, you must not beat yourself up for this. It is essential to be gentle with yourself. Beating yourself up will only cause you to turn into a spiral of negativity and continue to talk down to yourself. This will make you lose motivation and will make you feel like you are a failure. Having this state of mind will make it difficult not to turn to food for comfort. We must avoid this entire process by avoiding beating ourselves up in the first place. If we don't beat ourselves up and we instead encourage ourselves, instead of thinking of how we can't do it, and it is too hard and then needing to turn to food for comfort and a feeling of safety, we will not even make ourselves feel the need to find safety at all. Instead, we will talk to ourselves positively and encourage ourselves from within, which, instead of making ourselves feel bad, we will instead feel motivated, and we will be even more ready to continue on our journey.

Even if you don't fall off of the plan, it is still important to talk to ourselves nicely and with encouragement. We must recognize that changing our behaviors that we have likely been doing for some time is no small feat. We must encourage ourselves just like we would encourage someone else. Think of it as if you were talking to a good friend of a family member who was going through this instead of you. What would you say to them? How would you say it? You would likely be quite gentle and loving in your words. You would likely tell them that they were doing a great job and to keep it up. This is precisely how you want to speak to yourself from within and the exact types of words and phrases that you want to use. If we talked to our friends the way we talk to ourselves most of the time, they would be quite hurt. Thus, we must remember this when trying to motivate ourselves, and we must be gentle.

Another way to be gentle with yourself is to avoid being too restrictive in the beginning. You must understand that it will be a challenge, and easing into this new lifestyle will be best. Beginning by making small changes and then adding more and more changes as you go will be a good way for your mind and body to get used to the changes. If you dump a lot of changes on yourself too quickly, this will be quite a challenge for your mind and body.

How to Learn New Habits and a New Lifestyle

We have discussed some strategies for success so far in this chapter. Now, we will look at some ways to learn a new habit and ways to ensure your new lifestyle will stick.

Journal

The first method we will look at is journaling. Journaling can help in a process such as this because it can help you to organize your thoughts and feelings, and will help you to see visually what is working and what isn't working for you. While we can give tips and examples, every person is different, so to find exactly what works for you, you will have to try some different things and see which techniques help you personally the most and in the best way. Journaling can be about anything like how you feel since beginning a new program, how you feel physically since changing your diet, how you feel emotionally now that you are not reaching for food in order to comfort your emotions and anything along the lines of this.

Plan

Having a plan is key when it comes to succeeding in learning new habits and a new lifestyle. This plan can be as detailed as you wish, or it can be a general overview. I recommend in the beginning to start with a more detailed plan as you ease yourself into things. As everyone is different, you may be the type of person who likes lots of lists and plans, or you may be the type of person who doesn't, but for everyone, beginning with a plan and following it strictly for the first little while is best. For example, this plan can include things like what you will focus on each week, what you will reduce your intake of, and what you will try to achieve, and by when.

Meal Planning

Once you have come up with your general plan for your new lifestyle and how you want it to look, you can then begin planning more specifically. Planning your individual meals will make it much easier for you when you get home from work or when you wake up tired in the morning and need to pack something for your lunch. You can plan your meals out a week in advance, two weeks or even a month if you wish. You can post this up on your fridge, and each day, you will know precisely what you are eating, with no thinking required. This way, there won't be a chance for you to consider ordering a pizza or heating up some chicken fingers because you will already know exactly what you are going to make.

Grocery Shopping

As you are making a change to your diet, and your lifestyle surrounding food, the food you choose when grocery shopping makes a huge difference to your success. If you choose not to have the foods that you usually turn to in your house at all, you will not have the option to reach for it in a moment of weakness. By buying the alternatives to these things (like dried fruit instead of candy), you will be able to reach for something healthy if you must, or you may decide that you don't need a snack after all. If you don't give yourself the option of eating these things by not having them in your house, it will take much more effort to get them and this will likely discourage you at the moment, causing you to choose something healthier that is in the fridge already and ready to be eaten like a piece of fruit.

The other piece to this is that grocery list. When making your grocery list, it is important to make it in its entirety before going to the store. You do not want to go to the store without a list, as this will make it much more likely that you will come home with things that you didn't intend to buy or that don't fit into your new lifestyle. If you write out your entire list before you go, and take the time to write things that you will be able to eat without guilt, you can enter the store confidently and with a plan so that when you leave, you feel great about your progress. You can use the meal plan that you have made for your week to plan out your grocery list, and it will all be much easier this way. If you take out the in-the-moment decision making, this will remove a possible point for relapse.

The other point I want to make in regards to grocery shopping is that you want to avoid grocery shopping when you are hungry. If you enter the store when you are hungry and have not eaten dinner yet, regardless of whether you have a list or not, it will make it much harder to resist the snacks and the options that you routinely turn to when you are hungry and wanting a quick bite. If you are satiated, you will not be thinking of what you are craving at the moment, but what is on your list instead.

Doing all of these things with regards to grocery shopping are steps in the right direction and will make you feel proud of yourself.

Meal Prep

When it comes to trying to implement a lifestyle change or a new habit that involves food or dieting, meal prep will be a key to your success. Meal prep is when you prepare meals like your lunch or pieces to your dinner in advance so that you can easily prepare or reheat them later. You can meal prep an entire week's worth of lunches for yourself on the weekend, and all you would have to do in the morning before you leave for work or school is to take one out of the fridge. Then at lunch, you just pop it in the microwave, and you have a delicious and healthy lunch ready for you in under five minutes. You can prepare parts of your dinner in a similar way as well like preparing meat with a marinade the night before or cooking some chicken breast to reheat at dinner time.

The Weekly Cheat Meal

A weekly cheat meal is something that people may choose to include in their plan for their new lifestyle. As we discussed at the beginning of this chapter, a rigid approach has a lower chance of success than a gentle and positive-reinforcement technique or approach. The weekly cheat meal fits into this because it allows a person who has been working hard and following a plan a chance to reward themselves for their hard work and to ease up on pushing themselves for one meal. It can be quite tiring at first to think about what the healthy choice is and to wrestle with your cravings. Having one meal a week where you don't have to do this can help to refresh your mind and recharge you mentally so that you can enter another week with a strong mindset and dedication again.

The problem with the weekly cheat meal is that it can sometimes be extended into a cheat day or a cheat weekend, which is why it must be done with intention and restricted to one meal only. I recommend doing this on a Monday or during the midweek as it will be easier to pick up your new routine the next day if you are occupied with something like work or school and have your lunch prepared and ready to go in the fridge. If you do this on a Friday night, for example, it could pose a problem because this could begin by being a cheat meal on Friday for dinner, which could then turn into Friday night fast food after the bar when drunk, Saturday morning hangover food and so forth. Doing this on a Monday night would reward you after a weekend full of healthy choices and will help you continue on in the week with a healthy plan.

Chapter Conclusion

The strategies learned in this chapter will help you with anything you decide to take on in life, but especially food-related challenges. Now that we have learned about the different approaches to change and how to maintain a lifestyle change full of new habits, in the next chapter, we will look at hunger and the different forms it can take. You will find out how to read your hunger and how to decide when to eat.

Chapter 4: Hunger

In this chapter, we will look at the different types of hunger and how you can tell them apart. This will help you to distinguish when you are hungry and when you may be turning to food to soothe your emotional state.

Real Hunger vs. Perceived Hunger

It can be hard to tell sometimes when we are really hungry, and when we may be feeling as though food will make us feel better emotionally.

Real hunger is when our body needs nutrients or energy and is letting us know that we should replenish our energy soon. This happens when it has been a few hours since our last meal when we wake up in the morning, or after a lot of strenuous activity like a long hike. Our body uses hunger to signal to us that it is in need of more energy and that if it doesn't get it soon, it will begin to use our stored energy as fuel. While there is nothing wrong with our body using its stored fuel, it can be used as a sign to us that we should eat shortly in order to replenish these stores.

Perceived hunger is when we think we are hungry, but our body doesn't actually require any more energy or for the stores to be replenished. This can be because our brain notices that it is the time of day when we would normally eat. Even if we have just eaten a short time before, when we are feeling stressed or anxious, and our body isn't sure how to soothe this, we think that food may help. When our emotional state makes us crave comfort and good feelings, we—our brains—know that we can get this from certain foods like sugary or fatty ones.

How to Tell the Difference Between Real Hunger and Perceived Hunger

When we feel hungry, there are several questions we can ask ourselves to determine whether we are hungry and in need of sustenance, or we are hungry because of an emotional need. Below, I have listed the questions to ask and what they can tell us about our hunger.

1. When did I last have a meal?

We want to ask ourselves this question because if we had a full meal less than two or three hours ago, it is likely that we are not experiencing actual hunger. The hunger is coming from something else like an emotional need or boredom.

2. How hungry am I?

Go within and ask yourself how hungry you are. While you don't want to wait until you are absolutely starving and light-headed to eat, you want to be hungry enough.

If you are not quite at a level where you could eat a meal, you probably aren't hungry enough to eat just yet.

3. Am I still hungry now?

If you feel hungry, try drinking a glass of water. Wait twenty minutes and see if you are still hungry afterward. If you are not, you could have just been hungry because of your emotional state.

4. Was there a change in my emotional state just previously?

Sometimes, we will feel the need or the compulsion to eat right after we get some bad news or have an upsetting thought or conversation. Ask yourself if you felt the feeling of hunger directly after one of these occurrences or something that you know to be a trigger for your emotional hunger. If something like this has just happened, you may not have connected them as being related. By taking a minute to recognize this, you can decide that you may not actually be hungry and address the emotional issue instead.

Emotional Hunger Isn't Satiated With Food

5. Do I feel hungry again right after eating?

If we begin to eat or have a snack when we feel emotional hunger, you may feel good right afterward, but shortly after, it will not be resolved. This is another way to find out whether you are actually hungry or not. If you do decide to eat something and shortly after you feel hungry again, you were likely not hungry for food but had an emotional need instead. Since this emotional need could not be resolved with food, you feel famished and crave that positive feeling you get right after eating once again a short time later.

6. Do I feel guilty about eating?

If we eat when we are hungry, and after we feel satisfied and ready to continue on with our day, we will not feel any sense of guilt or shame about it since we were fueling our bodies. However, if we eat when we had a craving, and we felt hunger, but it was an emotional need telling us we were hungry, we may feel guilty or ashamed afterward about having eaten. This feeling can indicate that we were not really hungry but that we were trying to fill a void that was not filled by eating food.

The reason that hunger doesn't become improved or disappear after eating is that the body craves food for that positive feeling when getting after we eat. Like we talked about at the beginning of this book, eating certain foods or chemicals in food instead makes us feel rewarded and happy temporarily because of the reaction in our brain that is similar to taking a drug. Our mind enjoys this feeling, and it helps to lift our mood or take our mind off of our emotional turmoil for the time being. The problem is that when these rewarding and positive feelings are gone because the chemicals have gone away, we return to feeling the way we did beforehand. The only way to truly resolve our emotions or feel better about something is to face them head-on. Trying to solve them by other means like eating or distracting ourselves will only work in the short term and will leave us feeling the exact same way after the distraction is gone.

How to Eat

We will now look at some ways to improve our eating habits in order to make them healthier for us. When you ask yourself all of the above questions, and you determine that you are in fact hungry, there are ways to eat to ensure that you are making the most of the time that you are eating, while also getting all of the nutrients that you need when you are eating. We will talk about something called mindful eating. Mindful eating is when you really get into the moment, instead of being distracted by everything that is going on in your mind. If you are feeling down emotionally when you do decide that it is time to eat, you may be focused on your emotional state and not really tasting or enjoying the food that you are eating. By practicing mindful eating, you will be present in your eating experience. When you go to eat, do so sitting down on a chair with your food on a table in front of you. This will help with digestion and help you to form a routine around eating. Being sure to eat mindfully and without distraction will help you to digest better as well, which will help you to get all the nutrients you need from your food. Before you take a bite of your food, notice the smells of the food you are about to eat. Notice how it looks- the colors and textures. As you put food in your mouth, feel the textures of the food on your tongue. Notice all of the flavors that you are tasting and the feeling that they bring to your mouth. Notice how it feels when you chew the food- how it feels on your teeth and your cheeks. Doing this with every bite will bring you into the moment and ensure that you are consciously eating every time that you eat. Consciously eating will make you more aware of everything that you put into your mouth, and focusing on the experience of eating can help you to have fewer cravings and less desire to eat in between meals. Try practicing this every time you eat.

When to Eat

As I briefly mentioned earlier in this chapter, we want to eat when we are hungry, but not when we are ravenous. If we are only mildly hungry, we can likely stand to wait a little bit to eat. As a rule of thumb, when you start to become mildly hungry, begin to prepare your meal so that by the time you finish, you are the perfect level of hungry as you sit down to eat. If we wait to eat until we are absolutely ravenous, we will have let our blood sugar drop to quite a low level, and we will likely have begun to get light-headed, irritable, and have some difficulty with decision making. If you feel like this when you are starting to eat, you will want to make a note to eat a bit earlier next time. The sweet spot is about a level 5 of hunger on a one to ten scale.

How Much To Eat

It can be hard to know how much to eat and when you have had enough without going to the point where you have eaten too much and feel completely full. This section includes some tips on how much to eat so that you can begin to tell how much is the right amount for you.

When we eat, it takes about twenty minutes for the hormone in our bodies that tells us that we are full to reach our brain. Our stomach signals to our brain that we are hungry, and that signal takes about twenty minutes to reach the brain. Thus, we want to make sure that we eat slowly so that we can tell when we are full. If we eat very quickly, by the time we get the signal that we are full, we will have already eaten much more than we may have needed. Mindful eating will help you to eat slower than you normally might as you will be paying attention to each bite that you take. When you feel like you may be satiated, stop eating and wait for about twenty minutes. You will likely feel full then, but if not, you can always eat a bit more then.

Before you eat, drink a glass or so of water. This will help you to eat just the right amount and not too much, as this will help you to have something in your stomach already. This will also help with your digestion as the water will help everything to move smoothly along your digestive tract.

Guide to Meal Proportions

There is also a guide to the proportions of your meal. This guide helps us to determine the protein to carbohydrates to a vegetable ratio of each of our meals.

The reason why we want to keep track of this is that we want to make sure our meals are balanced. We don't want to have a plate that is 80 percent carbohydrates, or that is lacking in vegetables altogether. If we have a properly balanced plate, we will be giving our body everything it needs to function, and this will make it less likely that we will be hungry shortly after a meal, which is when we would be reaching for a snack. By giving our body the right amount of protein and vegetables mainly, this will keep us satisfied for longer, and then a snack will be the last thing on our minds. This helps to take care of one significant part of the emotional eating equation—if you are satisfied with your meal for longer, you will be less inclined to eat a snack even if you are feeling those nagging emotional needs.

Protein

When it comes to protein, we want to make sure we are eating enough of it because this is what keeps us full for longer. Protein takes longer to digest than carbohydrates; therefore, it gives us energy for longer. Remember the nutrient deficiencies we discussed in the second chapter of this book, eating lean proteins like a lean steak, chicken or turkey will help to give you the proper nutrients you need while keeping you full for longer on healthy and longer-lasting sources of energy. This will also help to combat the cravings that are indicative of a deficiency of some sort. When it comes to putting protein in your meal, you want the cooked and finished product to be roughly the size of your palm.

Carbohydrates

If you have ever had a meal or a snack that was largely composed of carbohydrates, especially the extremely processed kind, then you likely felt hungry again shortly after finishing. This is a big reason why meal composition is an important topic to become educated on. In today's societies, many of our meals will be mostly composed of carbohydrates, which is likely why many of us tend to remain hungry after a meal. When you are putting carbohydrates into your meal, you want the finished and cooked product to be about one handful worth.

Vegetables

When it comes to vegetables, many of us eat much less than we should. It is said that vegetables should make up half of your plate if you want to be an extremely healthy eater. What we will say here is that your meal should be composed of an amount of vegetables roughly the size of your fist, at minimum. The great thing about vegetables is that they occupy a lot of space for the amount of calories consumed, and they are also packed with nutrients. Adding an amount of vegetables that is larger than the size of your fist is going to fill you up without leaving you hungry a short time later and will also be giving you all of the nutrients you need to be a healthy individual. Remember the nutrient deficiencies we discussed in the second chapter of this book, eating many more vegetables will help to combat these cravings that are indicative of a deficiency of some sort.

Fats

When it comes to fats, not all of them are bad. We do not need to omit all fats from our diet as some of them are good fats that can actually help to lower the bad cholesterol and increase the good cholesterol. When we hear about fats and cholesterol, we tend to only hear about the bad kinds, which makes us afraid of fats altogether. However, we will look at this a little more, and you will see that there are some fat sources you can include in your diet in moderation. When it comes to adding fats to a meal, the rule is that you can have an amount of fat that is equivalent to the size of your thumb. You may be wondering what types of fats you can include in your diet that are not bad fats. Some examples of less desirable fats would include chocolate and fats from oils. The types of fat that you can include in amounts the size of your thumb include avocados, nuts like almonds, coconut oil, and other natural sources like this. The key to knowing which ones are to stick to the least amount of processing possible. The closest to the natural form that you would find in nature, the better.

With these guides that use your own hand as a tool, it accounts for different body sizes and body compositions. As you know, a tall man will need to eat more than a small woman. A tall man, however, will also have a bigger hand; therefore, a bigger fist, palm, and thumb, and their plate size will be bigger as well. This is a foolproof tool as this takes away any calorie counting, determining the weight and body composition or math needed to figure out the size that your meal should be. This makes it quick and easy and makes it so that anyone can do it anywhere. If you are at a restaurant, it will also help you to determine how much to eat and what you will order. Restaurant meals tend to be the worse culprits for including a disproportionate amount of carbohydrates and little to no vegetables. Keeping this in mind, you may decide to order a side of vegetables and pack up some of the carbohydrates in the meal to take home for lunch the next day.

In this chapter, we learned how, when, and how much to eat and how to tell what type of hunger you are feeling. We will now build on this by taking a closer look at emotional eating in the next chapter, so keep in mind everything you have learned in this chapter for the remainder of this book.

Chapter 5: Emotional Eating

In this chapter, we will look more in-depth at emotional eating in order to give you more information about what it is, why it occurs, and what could cause it. We will begin by once again defining emotional eating. Emotional eating occurs when a person suffering from emotional deficiencies of some sort including lack of affection, lack of connection, or other factors like stress, depression, anxiety or even general negative feelings like sadness or anger, eats or gives into food cravings that occur as a result of these emotional deficiencies in an effort to achieve feelings of comfort from the food they are eating.

How Food Cravings Can Indicate Emotional Deficiencies

You may be asking how food cravings can result from emotional deficiencies and how these two seemingly unrelated things can be considered related. While we have touched on this briefly in this book already, the reason for this is that your body over time learns that eating certain foods like those containing processed sugars or salts like fast food and quick pastries makes it feel rewarding, positive and happy for some time after it is ingested. When you are sad or worried, your body feels down and looks for ways to remedy this. Your brain then connects these two facts and decides that eating these foods will make it feel better. As a result of this process that happens in the background without you being aware of it, you then consciously feel a craving for those foods like sugary snacks or salty fast-food meals, and you may not even be aware of why. If you later decide to give in to this craving and eat something like a microwave pizza snack, your body will feel rewarded and happy for a brief period of time, which reinforces to your brain that craving food in an effort to make itself feel better emotionally has worked. If you end up feeling down and guilty that you ate something that was unhealthy, your brain will again try and remedy these negative emotions by craving food, and a cycle of emotional eating can then begin without you being any the wiser. Below is a visual display of the cycle of emotional eating.

The Cycle of Emotional Eating

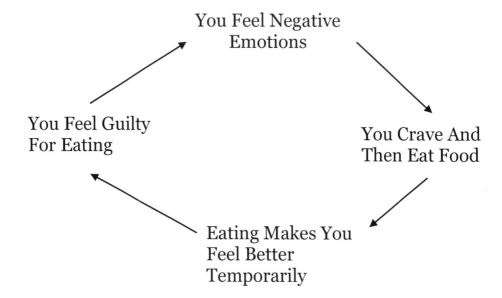

Because scientists and psychiatrists understand this process that occurs in the brain, they know that food cravings can indicate emotional deficiencies. While there are other types of cravings that can occur, such as those that pregnant ladies experience or those that show nutrient deficiencies, there are ways to tell that a craving is caused by emotional lacking of some sort. It begins by determining the foods that a person craves and when they crave them. If every time someone has a stressful situation, they feel like eating a pizza, or if a person who is depressed tends to eat a lot of chocolate, this could indicate emotional eating. If you crave fruits like a watermelon on a hot day, you are likely just dehydrated, and your body is trying to get water from a water-filled fruit that it knows will make it more hydrated. Examining things and situations like his leads scientists and psychiatrists to explore this concept in more depth and determine what types of emotional deficiencies can manifest themselves through food cravings in this way. We will look closer at these specific emotional deficiencies in the next section of this chapter.

Examples of Emotional Deficiencies

There are several types of emotional deficiencies that can be indicated by food cravings. We will explore these in detail below in hopes that you will recognize some of the reasons why you may experience struggles with eating.

Childhood Causes

The first example of an emotional deficiency that we will examine is more of an umbrella for various emotional deficiencies. This umbrella term is Childhood Causes. If you think back on your childhood, think about how your relationship with food was cultivated. Maybe you were taught that when you behaved, you received food as a reward. Maybe when you were feeling down, you were given food to cheer you up. Perhaps you turned to food when you were experiencing negative things in your childhood. Any of these could cause someone to suffer from emotional eating in their adulthood, as it had become something learned. This type is quite challenging to break as it has likely been a habit for many, many years, but it is possible. When we are children, we learn habits and make associations without knowing it that we often carry into our later lives. While this is no fault of yours, recognizing it as a potential issue is important to make changes.

Covering Up Emotions

Another emotional deficiency that can manifest itself in emotional eating and food cravings is actually the effort to cover up our emotions. Sometimes we would rather distract ourselves and cover up our emotions than to feel them or to face them head-on. In this case, our brain may make us feel hungry in an effort to distract us from the act of eating food. When we have a quiet minute where these feelings or thoughts would pop into our minds, we can cover them up by deciding to prepare food and eat, and convince ourselves that we are "too busy" to acknowledge our feelings because we have to deal with our hunger. The fact that it is hunger that arises in this scenario makes it very difficult to ignore and very easy to deem as a necessary distraction since, after all, we do need to eat in order to survive. This can be a problem, though, if we are not in need of nourishment, and we are telling ourselves that this is the reason why we cannot deal with our demons or our emotions. If there is something that you think you may be avoiding dealing with or thinking about or if you tend to be very uncomfortable with feelings of unrest, you may be experiencing this type of emotional eating.

Feeling Empty or Bored

When we feel bored, we often decide to eat or decide that we are hungry. This occupies our mind and our time and makes us feel less bored and even feel positive and happy. We also may eat when we are feeling empty.

When we feel empty the food will quite literally be ingested in an effort to fill a void, but as we know, the food will not fill a void that is emotional in sort, and this will lead to an unhealthy cycle of trying to fill ourselves emotionally with something that will never actually work. This will lead us to become disappointed every time and continue trying to fill this void with material things like food or purchases. This can also be a general feeling of dissatisfaction with life and feelings of lacking something in your life. Looking deeper into this the next time you feel those cravings will be difficult but will help you greatly in the long term as you will then be able to identify the source of your feelings of emptiness and begin to fill these voids in ways that will be much more effective.

Affection Deficiency

Another emotional deficiency that could manifest itself as food cravings is an affection deficiency. This type of deficiency can be feelings of loneliness, feelings of a lack of love, or feelings of being undesired. If a person has been without an intimate relationship or has recently gone through a breakup, or if a person has not experienced physical intimacy in quite some time, they may be experiencing an affection deficiency. This type of emotional deficiency will often manifest itself in food cravings as we will try to gain feelings of comfort and positivity from the good tasting, drug-like (as we talked about in chapter one) foods they crave.

Low Self-Esteem

Another emotional deficiency that may be indicated by food cravings is a low level of self-esteem. Low self-esteem can cause people to feel down, unlovable, inadequate, and overall negative and sad. This can make a person feel like eating foods they enjoy will make them feel better, even if only for a few moments. Low self-esteem is an emotional deficiency that is difficult to deal with as it affects every area of a person's life, such as their love life, their social life, their career life, and so on. Sometimes people have reported feeling like food was something that was always there for them, and that never left them. While this is true, they will often be left feeling even emptier and lower about themselves after giving into cravings.

Mood

A general low mood can cause emotional eating. While the problem of emotional eating is something that is occurring multiple times per week and we all have general low moods or bad days, if this makes you crave food and especially food of an unhealthy sort, this could become emotional eating. If every time we feel down or are having a bad day, we want to eat food to make ourselves feel better; this is emotional eating. Some people will have a bad day and want a drink at the end of the day, and if this happens every once in a while, it is not necessarily a problem with emotional eating. The more often it happens, the more often it is emotional eating. Further, we do not have to give in to the cravings for it to be considered emotional eating. Experiencing the cravings often and in tandem with negative feelings in the first place is what constitutes emotional eating.

Depression

Suffering from depression also can lead to emotional eating. Depression is a constant low mood for a period of months on end, and this low mood can cause a person to turn to food for comfort and a lift in spirit. This can then become emotional eating in addition to and because of depression.

Anxiety

Having anxiety can lead to emotional eating, as well. There are several types of anxiety, and whether it is general anxiety (constant levels of anxiety), situational anxiety (triggered by a situation or scenario), it can lead to emotional eating. You have likely heard of the term *comfort food* to describe certain foods and dishes. The reason for this is because they are usually foods rich in carbohydrates, fats, and heavy in nature. These foods bring people a sense of comfort. These foods are often turned to when people suffering from anxiety are emotionally eating because these foods help to temporarily ease their anxiety and make them feel calmer and more at ease. This only lasts for a short period of time; however, before their anxiety usually gears up again.

Stress

Stress eating is probably the most common form of emotional eating. While this does not become an issue for everyone experiencing stress, and many people will do so every once in a while, it is a problem for those who consistently turn to food to ease their stress. Some people are always under stress, and they will constantly be looking for ways to ease their stress. Food is one of these ways that people use to make themselves feel better and to take their minds off of their stress. As with all of the other examples we have seen above, this is not a lasting resolution, and it becomes a cycle. Similar to the cycle diagram we saw above, the same can be used for stress except instead of negative emotion and eating making you feel more down, stress eating can make you feel more stress as you feel like you have done something you shouldn't have which causes you to stress, and the cycle ensues.

There are many different emotional causes for the cravings we experience. There may be others than those listed above, and these are all valid. A person's emotional eating experience is unique and personal and could be caused by any number of things. You may also experience a combination of emotional deficiencies listed above, or one of those listed above in addition to others. Many of these can overlap, such as anxiety and depression, which are often seen together in a single person. The level of these emotional deficiencies that you experience could indicate the level of emotional eating that you struggle with. Whatever your experience and your struggles, though, there is the hope of recovery, and this is what the rest of this book will focus on. The next four chapters will explore techniques for recovering and will help you to form a plan that will work for you and your life.

Chapter 6: Emotional Eating Workbook

This chapter will include a workbook for your recovery from emotional eating and will help you to track your progress and plan your recovery journey. It will break this down into specific sections to ensure that every base is covered when it comes to your recovery.

Notes to Get Started

Now that you understand the reasons for and specific causes of emotional eating, you can begin your journey to changing your life for the better. Use this workbook as a tool for self-reflection. Doing some serious and deep self-reflection is not an easy process but a necessary one when it comes to healing yourself and changing your habits that are so ingrained. Looking deep within and asking yourself the proper questions will help you to take the first step, which is to acknowledge the issues and find the sources of them. Finding the sources will tell you precisely what you need to face and deal with in order to have a lasting change of lifestyle. If changing your ways is done as a distraction from the underlying issues, the change will not be lasting as these issues will rise to the surface again eventually, and they will manifest themselves in strong cravings. I want you to be able to change your life permanently, and in order to do this, we will begin with some deep self-reflection. You will get out of this workbook what you put in, so take your time as you go through this chapter and try to really get in touch with the deeper parts of yourself.

Self-Reflection

We will begin the self-reflection with some questions that you can ask yourself in order to get into a self-examination mindset.

Do I feel like I struggle with emotional eating?

Yes ____ No ____

Do I wish to find out the underlying causes of my emotional eating?

Yes ____ No ____

Do I feel like it is time for a lifestyle change in terms of my eating habits?

Yes ____ No ____

Pinpointing Your Emotional Deficiencies

In this section, we will continue our self-reflection by determining exactly what emotional deficiencies we are facing and struggling with, or what combinations of them. Doing this will help us to address these deficiencies and work on resolving them. There are various questions that you can ask yourself when pinpointing your emotional deficiencies.

Section 1

The first question you will ask yourself is a rather obvious one, but this will make it easy for you to get a start on your self-examination.

1. Have I been diagnosed with any mood-related disorders (such as depression, bipolar disorder, or anxiety)?

Yes ____ No____

If your answer is yes, you skip section 2. If you answered No and you are unsure if you suffer from one of these, complete section 2.

Section 2

1. Do I have lengthy periods of low mood or of an anxious state?

Yes _____ No _____

2. Have I been feeling this way for the last 3 to 6 months?

Yes _____ No _____

3. Do I often feel disconnected from my life?

Yes _____ No _____

4. Do I often feel nervous and worried about worst-case scenarios?

Yes _____ No _____

5. Do I often catastrophize in my head when thinking about things that are to come?

Yes _____ No _____

6. Do I often feel drastic swings between very high moods (happy, excited, motivated) and very low moods (sad, down, hopeless)

Yes _____ No _____

If you answered mostly Yes to the six questions above, you might suffer from a mood-related disorder. While this questionnaire is not conclusive and is not sanctioned by a doctor or a medical professional, this could give you a bit of direction when it comes to your mood, your emotions, and the causes of your emotional eating. Knowing that the cause could be something like depression, anxiety, or another mood disorder can help to give you some clarity on your own mental state. If you think this could be the case, consider visiting your doctor to talk about this further with someone who is especially knowledgeable in these areas.

Self-Ratings for Determining Emotional Deficiencies

Below, you will rate each of the emotional deficiencies that we discussed in the previous chapter on a scale from 1 to 10. Think about how much you feel each of these affects you and rate them accordingly. A rating of 1 on the scale means not at all or never, while a rating of 10 means all of the time, and a rating of 5 means half of the time.

1   5

10

Never   About half of the time   All of the
time/ Very frequently

Frequent changes in mood resulting in a need for comfort

1   2   3   4   5   6   7   8   9   10

Feelings of Boredom With Life

1   2   3   4   5   6   7   8   9   10

Feelings of Emptiness

1   2   3   4   5   6   7   8   9   10

Childhood habits and a learned unhealthy relationship
with food

1   2   3   4   5   6   7   8   9   10

Aiming to cover up your feelings and emotions

1   2   3   4   5   6   7   8   9   10

An Affection Deficiency

1   2   3   4   5   6   7   8   9   10

Low Self-Esteem

1   2   3   4   5   6   7   8   9   10

Depression

1   2   3   4   5   6   7   8   9   10

Anxiety

1   2   3   4   5   6   7   8   9   10

Generalized Feelings of Stress day-to-day

1   2   3   4   5   6   7   8   9   10

Your answers to the above questions will give you a visual guide to the most common emotional deficiencies in one place and will allow you to notice where you rate your level of each visually. This will allow you to see them all together and notice the ones that you feel you struggle with the most.

Food-Related Issues

This section of the workbook will look at the issues related to food and emotional eating specifically and how we can recognize and combat them.

Determining Your Emotional Deficiency Triggers

Now that we know what emotional deficiencies you are struggling with that cause you to emotionally eat, we will look at some more specific things or situations that trigger these issues for you, and that makes the emotional eating come about. Below is a worksheet where you will write down the triggers that you experience.

Situational Triggers

What are some triggers related to situations, scenarios, or experiences that exacerbate your emotional deficiencies and make them even stronger? For example: Going to the beach makes me recognize my low self-esteem more than usual.

Emotional Triggers

What are some triggers related to your emotions or specific emotions that make you seek comfort in the form of food? For example: When I feel scared, I begin to crave sweets.

Social Triggers

What triggers exist for you socially? For example: When I am out with friends, I feel pressured to act a certain way to fit in, and this makes me feel anxious.

Familial Triggers

What triggers, if any, are related to your family? These can be emotions, situations, or expectations. For example: When I am at home, I feel like nobody listens to me.

Other Triggers

Are there any other triggers that you experience that cause your emotional deficiencies to flare up? For example: When I go to school, I feel lonely

Recognizing your triggers is important because this will allow you to notice when you may be feeling emotional hunger and when you are feeling actual hunger. If you become hungry, you can look back on your day or the last hour and determine if any of your triggers were present. If they were, then you will be able to determine that you are likely experiencing emotional hunger, and you can take the appropriate steps instead of giving in to the cravings blindly. The way that these triggers can tie into emotional eating is because when you experience a trigger that causes one of your emotional deficiencies to become more apparent to you or to act up, this will be the time that you will be the most likely to turn to food as a means of comfort and as a way to self-soothe. Recognizing what these triggers are will help you to recognize when to intervene in your normal cognitive processes such as "I am hungry," "I am going to eat a cookie." Instead of this normal process that would occur after a situation or an emotion triggers your feelings of loneliness, for example, you will know to intervene, and instead, it will go something like this; "I am hungry," "Am I hungry or feeling an emotional need?", "A trigger just occurred, so I am going to call a friend and talk instead of eating what I crave."

We will now revisit some of the terms that we defined in the introduction to this book in order to determine how each of them does or does not play a role in your life. I have first defined them again as a refresher for you since we have learned a great deal since the introduction. For each of the statements below, rate how much you think you suffer from each on a scale from 1 to 10. A rating of 1 on the scale means not at all or never, while a score of 10 means all of the time, and a rating of 5 means half of the time.

1   5

      10

Never   About half of the time   All of the time/ Very frequently

1. Eating when I am feeling in a negative emotional state

Emotional Eating

1   2   3   4   5   6   7   8   9   10

2. Overeating is when a person eats more than they require in order to live and survive and when they

consume much more than they need in a day or in a single sitting. Overeating does not necessarily become binge eating, but it can.

Overeating

1   2   3   4   5   6   7   8   9   10

3. Binge eating disorder is when a person eats much more than a regular amount of food in a single sitting, and they feel unable to control themselves or to stop themselves once they begin.

Binge-Eating

1   2   3   4   5   6   7   8   9   10

4. Food addiction is a behavior that involves the consumption of foods that are high in fat, sugar, or salt. In other words, foods that taste great, as these will cause the person to feel rewarded by the consumption of these foods. This can be viewed similarly to drug addiction as the brain responds in the same way to these foods as it does to drugs.

Food Addiction

1   2   3   4   5   6   7   8   9   10

Now that you can see how each of these food-related behaviors affects you in your life, we can examine some ways in which recognizing these things will help you in your journey to recovery.

Recognizing Your Struggles Will Help Your Relationships

In this section, we are going to look at how recognizing your struggles will help your relationships. These relationships about which I speak are not just any relationships though, I am talking about your relationships with food, with your body and your mind. Now that we have spent some time on self-reflection and self-examination, you may be feeling a little bit down on yourself. However, I am here to tell you that doing this work can make you feel better about yourself! Recognizing the things with which you struggle will help you to decide what you want to do about them. Nobody can force anybody else to make a change, especially an entire lifestyle change. So recognizing the struggles that you are facing will allow you to be in charge of your journey to recovery and will let you decide the steps that you will take.

Food

As you can imagine from what we have discussed so far, recognizing the struggles you face such as your emotional deficiencies, the things that trigger them and the food-related issues that they cause, will allow you to begin to make changes in your habits and your lifestyle in order for you to start having a better relationship with food. Food can be seen as something that you need to survive, as a form of stress-relief through the cooking of healthy foods and as a way to bring people together. These examples, along with knowing when you are experiencing an emotional hunger, will allow you to change the way you approach food and will help you to avoid feeling guilty each time you feel that twinge of hunger in your body.

Body

Recognizing the food-related struggles you face will also help you to have a better relationship with your body. Instead of something that you dislike the shape of, something that causes you to feel hungry when you are not and guilty when you eat, and something that has disordered eating processes, you can begin to love it and care for it by providing it with nourishment, clean energy, and adequate hydration. Viewing your body as something to care for as it is the thing that carries you around all day and houses your most important parts will allow you to shift your view of yourself and your body and see it in a more positive light. You can begin to see it as something that you work together with instead of something that you work against.

Mind

Recognizing your struggles will also help you to have a better relationship with your mind. Understanding how your mind works will help you to better take care of it. You will be able to recognize your feelings and what they could be caused by, and then treat them in a way that will help it to feel better. Bettering your relationship with food and your body will also improve your relationship with your mind because you will begin to feed it what it needs, which will, in turn, lead to better cognitive functioning, control over impulses (like impulses to give in to cravings) and decision-making. This will help overall in your relationships with your food, your body, and your mind.

Specific Workbooks

To close this chapter, there are three workbooks that I want you to complete on an ongoing basis. These workbooks will help you to monitor your progress and will be a great tool to come back to over and over. It will be helpful to have this workbook filled out since the beginning of your journey for those days when you may be feeling discouraged and in need of some motivation. Looking back at your workbooks will help you to see how far you have come. They include topics like a food diary, some notes about your thoughts and feelings, and your goals. Copy the topics and questions listed below in each workbook into a notebook of your own where you can write as much as you like. Try to complete these questions each week or more, so that you will have enough information to monitor your progress as you go.

Food Workbook

In this workbook, you will keep a journal of your progress and your feelings toward your journey of improving your relationship with food.

1. How do I feel about this journey?
2. What are my goals for this journey with respect to food?
3. A food journal- journal about your meals, your progress and your thoughts/feelings about this

Body Workbook

In this workbook, you will keep a journal of your progress and your feelings toward your journey of improving your relationship with your body.

1. How am I feeling in regards to my body since beginning this journey?
2. What are my goals for this journey with respect to my body internally?

Mind Workbook

In this workbook, you will keep a journal of your progress and your feelings toward your journey of improving your relationship with your mind. There will also be some brainstorming involved to get you thinking in a solution-focused manner.

1. How will you deal with your emotions and struggles in other ways than eating

2. How you plan to intervene when you feel emotional hunger coming on

3. What steps will you take to change your relationship with your mind

4. What are your goals on this journey with respect to your relationship with your mind?

Chapter 7: Meal Plan

This chapter includes a meal plan to give you some ideas of things that you can eat and things that you should not eat. Begin by gradually making these changes and keep the tips that we talked about in chapter 3 in mind as you read through this meal plan.

Identify Micronutrient Deficiencies

As we discussed earlier in this book, cravings can indicate micronutrient deficiencies. These deficiencies can be identified by taking a blood test at your doctor's office. They will receive a print out from the lab they send your blood samples to and then return a list of all of the components of your blood and the levels of each. The doctor will then determine which of the micronutrients you are deficient in. With this information, you will be able to decide on those which you need to pay attention to the most, and you can, therefore, decide which foods you need to include in your diet.

We will look at some other ways to determine if you are deficient in some micronutrients. These ways to assess are not conclusive, and the best way to determine is through a blood test at the doctor's office. These ways will help you to determine what you will include in your diet and what you will look for more evidence of in your blood test.

Iron Deficiency

Symptoms of an iron deficiency include fatigue and lethargy, and weakness. If you generally feel tired and low on energy, the majority of the time, you are likely low on iron. This is a very common micronutrient deficiency. Iron deficiency can lead to anemia, which is a more serious form of iron deficiency, which leads to fatigue and weakness.

Magnesium Deficiency

You can recognize a deficiency in magnesium levels by muscle cramps and migraines. After a longer-term deficiency, it can also cause high blood pressure.

Iodine Deficiency

You can recognize this type of micronutrient deficiency by examining the area around the throat for an enlarged thyroid. It can also be recognized by increased weight gain and being short of breath.

Vitamin D Deficiency

A vitamin D deficiency takes longer to show itself than some others, but it can be identified by reduced immune system function as well as weak muscles.

Vitamin B12 Deficiency

As we discussed previously, anemia can also describe a low level of vitamin B12 and can be characterized by slower brain functioning, pale to yellow-colored skin, and fatigue.

We will now look at the best sources for each of these micronutrients that are the most commonly deficient in adults in the western world these days.

Sources of the Most Commonly Deficient Micronutrients

Sources of Iron

The best sources of iron are as follows;

- Red meat such as beef which can take many forms. The healthiest forms would be a lean steak or lean ground beef. This can also include pork.

- Meat from animal organs is also a good source of iron. This includes liver, kidney, brain, and heart meat.

- Shellfish are another excellent source of iron. These shellfish include clams, oysters, and mussels.

- Sardines are a good source of iron if you are in a hurry and don't have time to cook up a full meal. They will provide you with both protein and iron, even the canned variety.

- If you are a vegetarian, you can also get iron from some plant sources, though it will take much more volume to get the same amount of iron as you would from a serving of meat. Vegetarian sources of iron include beans, seeds like pumpkin or sunflower seeds, and leafy green vegetables like broccoli, kale, or spinach.

- Iron can be supplemented as well, but the healthiest sources are through whole foods like those described above as they are natural, and most of them will provide the body with other benefits as well as iron, like protein.

Sources of Magnesium

- Whole grains are a great source of magnesium. This can include whole grain oats or bread
- Nuts like almonds or cashews provide dietary magnesium as well.
- Dark chocolate, as we saw earlier in the book, is a good source of magnesium.
- Green leafy vegetables are a great source of magnesium. The darker green vegetable, the better. Examples include spinach and kale.

Sources of Iodine

- Seaweed is a good source of iodine. Seaweed can be consumed in a dried form, as a seaweed salad or as kelp in soups.
- Fish is another good source of iodine. Fish has numerous benefits to our health, one of which is providing a good source of iodine.
- Dairy sources can also provide iodine in your diet. This includes yogurt, cheese, and milk.

- Eggs are another source of iron, as well as a good source of protein.

Sources of Vitamin D

There are not many foods with high levels of Vitamin D, so these must be consumed in addition to a supplement or simply increasing your exposure to the sun. The following foods are the best dietary sources of Vitamin D:

- Fish that are higher in fat such as salmon, sardines, and trout contain a good amount of dietary vitamin d.
- Egg yolks get a bad reputation because of cholesterol, but they are one of the few sources of vitamin d
- Cod liver oil can be taken as a supplement for vitamin D as an alternative to vitamin D in pill form.

Sources of Vitamin B12

- Vitamin B12 is only found in high quantities in animal products. The only known source that is from plants is found in seaweed in small amounts.,
- Shellfish is high in vitamin B12 like clams oysters and mussels

- Organ meat is also a good source of vitamin B12.

- Meat as a general category is another great source of vitamin B12. The best sources can be lean steak, turkey, or chicken breast.

- Eggs and milk products are two other good sources of vitamin B12. Drinking milk and eating a whole egg will provide you with some vitamin B12.

Macronutrients

We will now look at the macronutrients. We just looked at micronutrients, which are the small vitamins and minerals that makeup macronutrients, which include protein, carbs, vegetables, and fats. The best sources of any macronutrients will be those natural sources. So this is what we will focus on here.

Protein

The best sources of protein are always going to be the leanest and most natural sources. The less lean forms of meat protein contain lots of animal fat, which is not the good kind of fat we are looking for. We will revisit fats later on, but for now, we are going to take a look at lean sources of protein.

- Lean meats include turkey, chicken, lean beef and fish

- Eggs are a good source of protein as well as dairy sources like milk and cheese. Greek yogurt has a lot of protein and can be bought without added sugar, making it a good choice for a healthy snack.

- You can also get protein if you are a vegetarian from non-animal sources like tofu, beans, lentils, and other legumes.

Carbohydrates

Believe it or not, there are actually many, many natural sources of carbs. Most of the time, when we think of carbohydrates, we think of bread, pasta, and quick foods. However, did you know that fruits and vegetables are actually an excellent source of carbohydrates? Examples of good carbs in the form of fruits and vegetables include bananas, strawberries, and apples as well as cabbage, broccoli, carrots, and so on and so on. There are no vegetables that should be avoided; any of them are a good source of healthy carbs.

- Potatoes and sweet potatoes are good sources of carbohydrates in a healthy way.

- Other examples of natural and good carbohydrates include seeds like pumpkin or sunflower, nuts like almonds, hazelnuts, walnuts, and peanuts (if unsalted), legumes like beans, peas, and lentils.

- When it comes to those bread sources, you think of right away, and only those whole grains are included in the more natural and healthy carbohydrate sources. Examples include brown rice, whole grain oats, quinoa (which is also very high in protein), truly whole-grain bread as many pieces of bread are just refined flour slices of bread colored brown to trick us. Make sure you check the ingredients list to ensure it is actually whole grain bread, the fewer ingredients, the better.

Vegetables

We already discussed vegetables above, but they are also usually included in their own category when it comes to planning meals. Vegetables should be included in every meal in n small proportion because of their numerous health benefits. These benefits include all of the vitamins and minerals that we need and tend to be deficient in, as we saw above, as well as their low-calorie content for such great volume. Vegetables are an excellent source of natural carbohydrates as well as excellent sources of so many other things.

Fats

As we discussed earlier, there are good fats that are not the same as those fats that you have heard of as being bad for you. These good fats come from whole food sources and are not the same as the saturated fats that you find in quick foods. Sources of these healthy fats include:

- Avocados are a great source of healthy fats, as we have seen previously in this book.
- Cheeses are another great source. Stick to the most natural cheeses you can find, such as mozzarella, blue cheese, parmesan cheese, and swiss cheese, for example. The reason cheese is so healthy is because of the good fats it contains, which have been shown to reduce the risks of disease.
- Nuts are another source of good fats as well as fatty fish like salmon, whole eggs, and dark

chocolate. All of these contain natural and unprocessed fats that can be good for our health when consumed in moderation (remember the thumb rule of plate composition)

- Extra virgin olive oil is another source of good fats and is one of the few oils we should use for cooking. We can omit vegetable oil, soybean oil, and canola oil, among others. Coconut oil is another great source of good fats, and this can be used in so many things like coffee, smoothies, baking, and a pan greaser.

Identify Your Personal Cravings

In this section we will identify some of your personal cravings when it comes to food and those common cravings you get in times of stress of anxiety. Below, write some of these cravings down for yourself to refer to later on. Be as specific as possible for yourself.

_____

_____

_____

_____

_____

_____

_____

_____

_____

_____

_____

_____

_____

We will look at some common cravings that people will experience in times where they need comfort or to lift their mood.

- Chocolate bars
- Muffins
- Potato chips
- Pastries like doughnuts or croissants
- French fries
- Fast-food hamburgers
- Ice cream
- Cake or cupcakes

- Candy like gummy bears
- Soda pop
- Popcorn

Easy Food Swaps

We have discussed some swaps previously for foods that you crave, and here we will visit a few more examples;

If you are craving a chocolate bar, try gradually switching over to a 70 percent dark chocolate. This may take some time, but begin with your usual and switch to a higher and higher percentage of dark chocolate. You will still be getting your chocolate fix, but it will be in a healthier way that will be more beneficial for your health.

If you are craving soda pop, try beginning with some sparkling water or tonic water and add some fruits into it to give it some flavor. This may taste odd at first, but it will still give you the fizzy feeling in your mouth, and you will be getting some sugar from the fruit, but they will be natural sugars instead of refined sugars.

If you are craving french fries or potato chips, try baking some potatoes or sweet potatoes in the oven drizzled with some olive oil and lightly salting them so that you can have a very similar taste to the french fries or chips, but much less processed and with fewer additives.

If you are craving ice cream, try putting some fruits into the freezer in advance and then blending them into a smoothie. If they are not already frozen, you can add some ice when you blend the fruit. You can add some plain greek yogurt for added protein and don't blend it too much so that it is still a little chunky like ice cream is. Then put it into a bowl and eat it with a spoon.

Now, try doing the same for the foods you wrote down in the previous section, if they are different from the examples above.

_____

_____

_____

_____

_____

_____

_____

_____

_____

_____

_____

_____

Meal Ideas

In this section, I will give you some meal ideas for things that you can make yourself at home. It can be daunting knowing where to begin, but this guide will help you get started.

Snacks, Desserts, Treats

In the previous section, when we looked at food swaps you can make to avoid giving in to cravings, we looked at a few examples of things you could eat instead of the chocolate or the french fries that you craved. These examples included baked potatoes, a smoothie bowl, dark chocolate, and sparkling water flavored with fruits. These are great examples for when you decide that what you are experiencing is genuine hunger and not an emotional hunger, and you want to have something that is healthier than those convenience foods that we often reach for in moments of hunger.

Fruit is a good example of a dessert that you can have after your meal if you are still hungry. If you want a little bit of sweetness after your meal, save room for some fruit like watermelon, strawberries, or raspberries, and you will get your sugar fix in a completely natural way.

Breakfast

For breakfast, some people do not enjoy eating savory foods. For those people, I recommend plain Greek yogurt to give you protein first thing in the morning and get you going, with a little bit of honey and some fruits added in for natural sweetness.

You could also have some whole grain granola mixed with fruit and yogurt or with milk.

For those who enjoy savory breakfast, having some sautéed spinach with a couple of boiled eggs and a slice of whole-grain toast is the best option. If you want some meat as well, you can make some sausage patties out of lean ground turkey and cook those to add in. Feel free to switch the spinach for any other vegetable and either roast it in the oven or sauté it with some garlic and olive oil.

Lunch

For lunch, preparing your meals in advance is a great way to ensure you will be eating healthy while still having something quick to grab and pop into the microwave. In advance, cook up some chicken or turkey breast or a fillet of fish. Mix this with a vegetable of your choice (roughly the size of your fist) and some potatoes or sweet potatoes.

If you have more time for lunch, you can make yourself some quinoa, which is high in protein but is also a carbohydrate, as well as a variety of vegetables diced and mixed in, and finish it off with some protein like tofu or chicken.

Dinner

For dinner, make yourself a platter of healthy tacos using corn tortillas, homemade salsa, some homemade guacamole (both homemade so you can see exactly what is going into it and control the amounts of salt) as well as some pan-seared fish filets. There you will have a healthy fish taco platter. As a side, boil or grill some corn on the cob and season it with a bit of cayenne pepper for a little added spice.

Another idea is to make stuffed peppers. Cut one red, green, or yellow bell pepper in half and fill it with some cooked lean ground beef, some vegetables of your choice like corn, for example, some salsa and top with mozzarella. Then, bake the two halves in the oven, and you have a delicious and healthy dinner made.

When it comes to meal planning, it can be simple. Just substitute the protein, carbohydrates, or vegetables, and you have a new meal. This will take the invention work out of it and will keep you from getting bored. Knowing what you know now about food and healthy choices, you can also scour the internet or cookbooks for recipes that you'd like to try. If they seem like they may not be that healthy, try substituting them with healthier options or looking up healthier alternatives of the same dish on the internet. The internet is full of amazing recipes for you to explore!

Chapter 8: Exercise

Exercise has been proven to help with a variety of things in life, such as stress, impotence, and general health. Emotional eating is no different. Exercise is excellent for our body, our mind, and our overall health. Adding an exercise regime into your life is as important, if not more, than any other measures you take to maintain your health.

How Exercise Will Help You in Recovery

Exercise will help you in your journey to recovery because of the many ways that it affects our different body systems. As you know, all of our body systems work together to form the person that we are. If one of them isn't functioning quite as well as it should be, all of the other systems feel it too. Exercise works on all of these systems at the same time, and if one of them isn't firing on all cylinders, exercise will help that system to wake up, improve, and to stay healthy. Exercising while on this process to recovery will aid in keeping you feeling strong when it may be getting tough. Exercising will show you what your body can do and how strong it is, which in turn will make you feel stronger mentally. Exercising will help you take your mind off of those nagging cravings, and will give you a clearer mind overall with which you can look deep inside at those cravings and the emotional issues that are causing them. Exercise will help in all aspects of your life and will help you to continue reaching for recovery.

How Exercise Affects Mood and the Brain

When we exercise, our brain releases chemicals that tell us that we enjoy the effects that the exercise is giving us. This feeling is known as "runner's high," and it is that happiness you feel after you run a long-distance or complete a workout. When you are feeling down, and you exercise, your mood will lift because of this runner's high. This process is similar to the process that we discussed at the beginning of this book, whereby the release of chemicals in the brain is triggered by the molecules of the highly processed foods that we like to ingest. This runner's high can be compared to those rewarded feelings that the highly sugary foods give us, but with runner's high, the sense of elation and accomplishment last way longer than the rewarded happy feelings we get from eating food. Industrial food makes our brains feel happy, but our body feels heavy and lethargic. Exercise, as I mentioned, makes all of our body parts feel great at the same time, and this is why the effects of runner's high are so long-lasting.

When you feel an emotional craving for food coming on, acknowledge it, examine the deeper feelings behind it, and question them a little bit. Once you have done this, go for a run or complete a workout of some sort. This will not only make you feel great because you didn't give into the craving (so you don't feel the guilt) and you have overcome the craving, but you will also feel that runner's high, a lifted mood, the strength that your body is capable of and the satisfaction of feeling all of these things at once.

Exercise affects the brain in other chemical ways, as well. When we exercise, our heart rate increases, as you know. What this does is carry more oxygen to our muscles so that they can keep exercising. It also carries more oxygen to our brains. More oxygen and blood flow to the brain means that your brain will work more efficiently, more sharply, and with more clarity, after you finish exercising. More blood flow to the brain also means that it will be generally healthier. Exercising often and for a continuous period of time helps to keep the brain structures themselves healthy and in working order. This helps with memory, decision making, and learning.

Exercise has been shown to be the most effective antidepressant. Many pills are prescribed to treat and beat depression, but the most effective and most natural way to continually boost your mood and to keep it up is through exercise. The effects that exercise has on the brain are far-reaching and numerous.

How Exercise Affects the Body

When we exercise, we become stronger, faster, and more agile. This not only helps us to exercise better but it helps us in our everyday lives. Moving through life with more ease than before is a great feeling that can only be achieved through exercise. Our bodies are built to move, and they love it when we do move! Our bodies are built to become stronger with the more we do continually, and this is what inevitably happens as soon as we begin exercising regularly. You can start to see aesthetic changes, as well. You can see your muscles growing, your body toning, and your fat disappearing. These changes on the inside and the outside make us feel great about the body we live in and about the progress we are making mentally. Taking the time to go to the gym and exercise and stick with an exercise program shows our body that we are willing to do the hard work that exercising takes, and it also shows our mind the same thing.

Exercise Examples and Samples

What defines exercise to you all depends on your regular state. Your state of being on a day to day basis determines what your body is used to. Exercising is pushing your body physically past what it is used to in a cardiovascular sense, in a strength sense, and in an endurance sense, among others. If you are used to sitting down all day and driving a car everywhere, exercise to your body may look like walking to the store on the weekend instead of driving, or walking up the stairs instead of waiting for the elevator. Exercise meets you where you are, and your brain will gladly take any form of the new movement as a mood booster. Below we will look at some sample exercises for any level of a mover.

Sedentary

If you usually don't do much exercise or much walking around, begin by taking the stairs sometimes. Begin also by deciding to walk some places, like to the store down the street or if there is nothing like that around, do some walking around your block. Beginning with this type of movement will get your body used to moving again and will get your muscles and joints moving smoothly.

Occasional Mover/Walker

If you walk occasionally like to a bus stop or to the store on your lunch break, you can begin with a little bit more exercise than someone who is sedentary. Since your muscles and joints are likely somewhat used to being in a standing position, you can begin to jog a little bit. You can jog after dinner around the block a few times, or jog to the store and walk back every few days. You could also take a yoga class if you wish or do some video-guided yoga at home.

Moderate Walker/ Casual Mover

If you have a moderate level of walking included in your life and you occasionally speed that up to a jog, you can begin to move your body around in new and different ways. Try doing some sit-ups and push-ups at home before or after your run, or run to the park and use the playground equipment to do some chin-ups, some two-foot jumps onto a step or run up and down the steps a few times. This will keep your heart rate up and teach your body new ways of moving while allowing your upper body muscles to get a bit of attention as well.

Casual Mover/ Moderate Runner

If you run frequently and have some bodyweight exercise sessions every now and again, try visiting a gym and doing some exercises with some more weight. You can try squatting, pressing some things overhead, and maybe some bicep curls. This will challenge your muscles in ways that your own body weight cannot and take you to a new level of fitness and mood-boosting.

Experienced Runner

If you are an experienced runner, you are likely quite familiar with the feeling of runner's high. You are probably quite familiar with how exercise can change your mood around and take you from feeling hopeless to hopeful. If you want to try some new forms of exercise, try adding in a regular routine in the gym lifting weights. This will take your running to new heights and will give you a new type of exercise experience to break up the running days.

Experienced Exerciser

If you are experienced when it comes to exercise, good for you! Continue to challenge yourself in new ways and teach your body new ways of moving. Exercise does nothing but good things, so keep up your routine.

For any level of exerciser or mover, challenging your body in new ways will be beneficial in so many aspects of your life. In addition to its effects on the brain, body, and mood, it will help with your health in the long-run and the ease with which you will be able to complete everyday tasks like climbing the stairs and throwing a ball to your child. The goal is to make this a part of the new lifestyle we are working towards, which will make it so ingrained in your life that you will not want to go without it.

Chapter 9: Willpower and Motivation

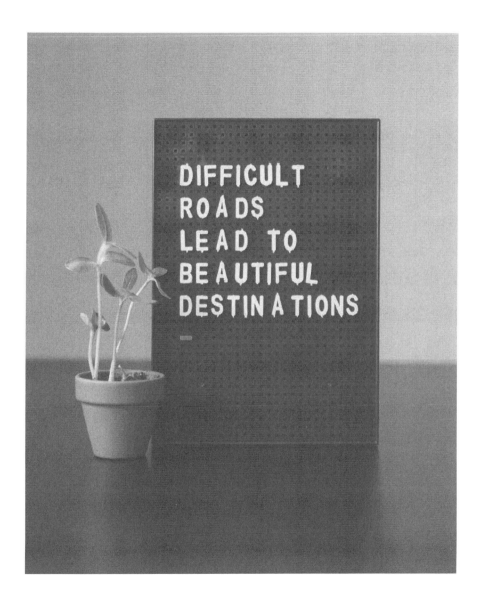

Now that you have learned all of the components to changing your life for the better when it comes to emotional eating, I am going to leave you with some tips to make sure that you can stay on track and achieve your goals. One of the keys to this that I want to begin with is going into it with the goal of combining everything you have learned and want to accomplish into one new lifestyle for yourself. This will include your new meal plans, your new snack options, and choices, your continued work on your relationship with food and with yourself, as well as regular exercise. As you begin, it will be difficult, but ease your way into it. And once these all become habits, you won't even notice that you are doing them anymore, and they will become second nature. Anything can become a habit if we practice it for long enough, and these lifestyle changes are no different.

What to Do When It Becomes Difficult

It is inevitable when trying to accomplish something as big as making a change to something that is ingrained in your life- like eating, that it will become difficult at some points along the way. This section will look at what we can do when it becomes difficult.

The first thing that you should do is expect it to become difficult at some point. Going into this journey, expecting that it will be a breeze, will only leave you feeling like you have done something wrong when a hard day or a tough week surprises you. If you go into this if the mindset that it will become difficult at least a few times, will prevent this from surprising you when it happens and will allow you to appropriately deal with it instead of wondering what you did you cause it.

When it becomes difficult, and you don't know what to eat, you are in a rush, and you have no groceries left, the first thing you want to do is take a deep breath. Then, remind yourself why you started in the very first place. Think back on your old ways and how they made you feel. Think of where you are now and praise yourself for what you have accomplished so far- no matter how small. Then, go to the fridge and eat one of the lunches you had intended to take for work tomorrow. By tomorrow, you will likely be having a better day and will have regrouped with your old willpower restored, which will allow you to make a good and healthy decision for your lunch.

Don't get discouraged when something arises that challenges you on your journey. Take it as it comes and tell yourself that this is just what happens in life. Nothing comes without challenges. Like we talked about earlier in this book, if something comes up that causes you to slip up and eat something that you would otherwise have chosen not to, don't beat yourself up; just continue on with your plan and continue as you would have at the next meal.

Motivation Tips

When you lack motivation, it will help to write about this in your workbook. While you are there, also look back at your previous notes in the workbook and look at the progress you have made. Sometimes when things become a habit, we forget that they didn't use to be. Think about some of the things that are habits of yours now that were not habits of yours a year ago. This will remind you of what you are able to accomplish.

Reach out to someone who is supporting you that can provide you with some words of encouragement. This could be anyone who you trust and who you know has your best interests at heart. They will be able to give you some words to motivate you and keep you on track.

Look to support centers online for people recovering from emotional eating or other food-related issues. This can help you to feel that you are not alone and that there are many other people facing similar challenges. This will motivate you to keep pushing.

How to Work on Willpower

Willpower is something that is hard to pinpoint, but that is somewhere within all of us. We have to find it somewhere within, and it is there! Think of someone or some people who you think demonstrate great willpower. Ask yourself what about them shows this. Ask yourself how you think they do this (don't reply with "they just have it"). Ask yourself what other qualities they possess that you admire. Ask yourself if you can pull those same qualities from within yourself. Thinking in this way and trying to emulate a person you admire and respect will help you to know precisely how willpower looks to you and how willpower displays itself in a person. Having something more concrete to work towards or to reference will help you to find your own willpower that is within you.

How to Stick to the Diet

The key to sticking to the diet is one word: *preparation.* Being prepared for anything will ensure that you won't be able to give yourself any excuse to fall off of the diet. For example, doing all of the following:

- Meal prep your lunches.
- Find a place to buy a healthy lunch near your work or school, just in case you forget your lunch one day.
- Prepare a menu for your dinners for the week each weekend.
- Don't buy the snacks that you would usually crave at the grocery store.
- Grocery shop with a specific list and when you are not hungry.
- If you are going out socially, pre-plan what you will order and the number and type of drinks you will have. Then stick to this.

Doing all of the above things will make it almost impossible to not stick to the diet. Because everything will be prepared for you already, all you have to do is move the fork to your mouth at every meal, and the diet is stuck to!

How to Reward Yourself as You Hit Milestones

Rewarding yourself is important as you make your way through this difficult journey. When you hit milestones like *one month on the diet* or *one month without giving in to a craving*, then you will keep yourself motivated because you will be working toward your next milestone and, therefore, your next reward each day. Leave enough space between rewards; otherwise, they won't feel as special. Reward yourself once per month at first and then once every few months as you get more used to everything. You can reward yourself by allowing yourself to buy a medium popcorn at the movie theatre after you have exercised three times a week for a month, for example.

Plan your rewards and write them down on a calendar so that if you are feeling a lack of motivation, you will be able to look at the visual and see how close you are to achieving that goal and that reward. We as creatures love to be rewarded and love to accomplish goals and so giving yourself these options will help you to achieve them.

Conclusion

We are going to talk about how to maintain personal growth. You may be scared that even if you can do these things for a little, that you may relapse and have a tough time getting ahold of yourself again. By following each of these tips listed in this chapter, you will be able to hold yourself accountable, keep yourself motivated, and reward yourself when you do. Keep this book handy so that you can look back at any chapter and give yourself a reminder of any topic. Look at your old workbooks and pat yourself on the back. Practice these things like diet and exercise every single day so that they become second nature. With all of the self-reflection and self-examination that you have done and that you continue to do, lasting change is very, very likely. If you were simply covering up your food issues by trying a new diet, the chances of lasting change would be slim. However, if you look deep inside and question your habits and your behaviors, you will never be able to blindly give into cravings without first examining and questioning them like you have learned to do in this book. Further, once you get to a certain point in your journey, you will not allow yourself to relapse because of how far you've come and how much work you have put in. Continue on in this process with confidence and with a one-track mind.

Thank you for reaching the end of this book. I hope that you have learned a great deal about the foods we usually eat, the reasons why we crave them, and what other options we have. I also hope that you have learned a lot more about yourself. This book involved a lot of self-reflection, and you should be proud of yourself for completing these exercises that may have been difficult. Facing these parts of ourselves is never easy, but it is the necessary work that must be done in order for lasting change to occur.

Your next steps are to continue to examine yourself every day. Question why you do things and what is behind them. Approaching your life in this way, even other aspects of your life, will make you a self-reflective and emotionally intelligent person. This self-awareness will not only benefit you in your own life but in your relationships with others as well.

This process will end up teaching you more about yourself than you realize, and will hone your willpower and your self-control skills which will carry over into every part of you.

By reading this book, you have already taken a step in the right direction, and you are already on your way to becoming a changed person for the better. With the things you know about food, diet, and exercise, you can share this with the people you care about who may be suffering from emotional eating as well. If you have a family, introduce these techniques and this knowledge to your kids so that you can all take these steps to change together.

Made in the USA
Monee, IL
10 March 2025

13836093R00090